The Open University

MST125

Essential mathematics 2

Unit 12

Combinatorics

This publication forms part of an Open University module. Details of this and other Open University modules can be obtained from the Student Registration and Enquiry Service, The Open University, PO Box 197, Milton Keynes MK7 6BJ, United Kingdom (tel. +44 (0)845 300 6090, email general-enquiries@open.ac.uk).

Alternatively, you may visit the Open University website at www.open.ac.uk where you can learn more about the wide range of modules and packs offered at all levels by The Open University.

To purchase a selection of Open University materials visit www.ouw.co.uk, or contact Open University Worldwide, Walton Hall, Milton Keynes MK7 6AA, United Kingdom for a brochure (tel. +44 (0)1908 858779, fax +44 (0)1908 858787, email ouw-customer-services@open.ac.uk).

FSC www.fsc.org MIX Paper from responsible sources FSC® C013436

The Open University, Walton Hall, Milton Keynes, MK7 6AA.

First published 2015.

Edited, designed and typeset by The Open University, using the Open University TEX System.

Printed in the United Kingdom by Latimer Trend and Company Ltd, Plymouth.

ISBN 978 1 4730 0319 4

1.1

Contents

Introduction

Combinatorics is the term used to describe the mathematics of counting. A *counting problem* is one that asks 'how many ...?', or 'count the number of ways of ...'.

The name 'combinatorics' is related to the word 'combinations': often a good approach to a counting problem is to divide it up into parts that are easier to count, and then to *combine* the results to get the final answer.

In this unit, you'll be introduced to a number of key ideas in combinatorics. In Section 1, you'll meet three fundamental principles of counting – the *multiplication principle*, the *addition principle* and the *subtraction principle* – and learn how to use them to solve counting problems such as:

> How many positive integers less than 1000 do not contain the digit 1 in their decimal representations?

Section 2 covers three more important concepts – *sequences*, *permutations* and *combinations* – before concluding with a short diversion into probability theory, where you'll find out how to answer the following question:

> What is the probability of winning the UK National Lottery?

The remainder of the unit is devoted to investigating methods for finding and solving recurrence systems, which were introduced in MST124 Unit 10. A *recurrence system* is a way of specifying a sequence by giving the initial term or terms of the sequence, and an equation that shows how each subsequent term in the sequence depends on the previous terms (the *recurrence relation*).

In Section 3 you'll meet a number of examples of *first-order* recurrence systems, where each term in the sequence depends on the immediately preceding term but no others. The examples you'll see include the calculation of mortgage repayments, and the following question from geometry, which is illustrated in Figure 1.

> If n infinite straight lines are placed in the plane, in such a way that each two lines meet but no three lines intersect at a single point, into how many regions is the plane divided?

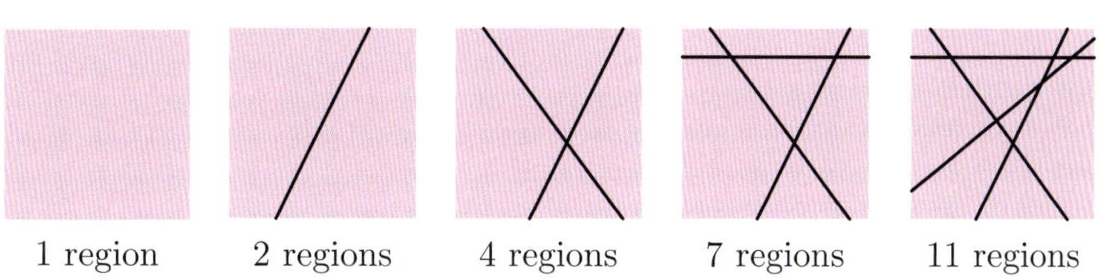

Figure 1 The number of regions in the plane when it is divided using 0, 1, 2, 3 or 4 infinite straight lines

Finally, in Section 4, we look at *second-order* recurrence systems, where each term in the sequence depends on the preceding *two* terms. Our study will be motivated by the *Fibonacci sequence* (F_n), which begins $1, 1, 2, 3, 5, 8, 13, \dots$, and is given by the recurrence system

$$F_1 = 1, \quad F_2 = 1, \quad F_n = F_{n-1} + F_{n-2} \; (n = 3, 4, 5, \dots).$$

This famous sequence arises in many counting problems, including one posed by Leonardo of Pisa (Fibonacci) in 1202 AD about counting the number of pairs of rabbits as they breed, month by month.

The word 'combinatorial' was first used in its current mathematical sense by Gottfried Wilhelm Leibniz (1646–1716) in his *Dissertatio de arte combinatoria* ('Dissertation concerning the combinational arts') of 1666.

1 Principles of counting

In this section, you'll be introduced to three fundamental principles of counting by studying a variety of typical counting problems.

Counting problems sometimes involve counting physical objects, but more often they are about counting the number of ways of doing something. For example, they may be about the number of ways of performing a task that has several steps, or of making a series of choices one after another, or of organising a collection of items in some given pattern. In general, when we refer to 'objects', we mean whatever is being counted in our particular problem, which may well not be physical objects. The range of mathematical problems that involve counting is vast, and you'll meet several different types in this unit.

Many of the techniques for solving counting problems are best described using the idea of *sets*, which were introduced in MST124 Unit 3. You'll learn more about sets as the counting problems you meet increase in complexity.

1.1 The multiplication principle

Consider the following counting problem.

Example 1 *Counting the number of three-course meals*

A café has the following menu, where (v) indicates a vegetarian option:

Starters Paté and toast Baked camembert (v)
Mains Chicken salad Penne pasta with tomato and basil sauce (v) Mushroom and cheese omelette (v)
Desserts Apple tart (v) Iced Chelsea bun (v)

How many different three-course meals are possible?

Solution

We need to find a systematic way of counting every possible three-course meal, so that none is counted more than once and none is missed out. A *tree diagram* is a good way of doing this. Each three-course meal is represented by a path from the top of the tree diagram (which is labelled 'Start') to one of the nodes at the bottom (in this case, each labelled 'Tart' or 'Bun').

The options from the menu can be illustrated by the following tree diagram.

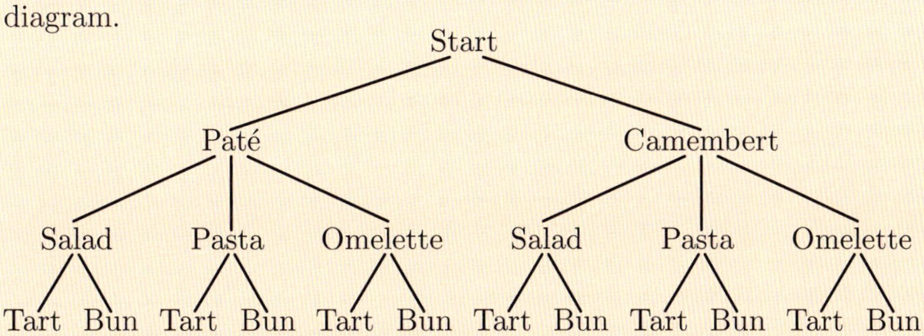

The number of different three-course meals is equal to the number of paths from the top of the tree diagram to the bottom, and this is equal to the number of nodes along the bottom row.

There are 12 nodes along the bottom of the tree diagram, so there are 12 possible three-course meals.

Notice that the tree diagram in Example 1 tells you more than just the number of possible three-course meals. By following each of the different paths from the top to the bottom of the tree diagram, you can also list the twelve possible meals:

Paté, Salad, Tart
Paté, Salad, Bun
Paté, Pasta, Tart
Paté, Pasta, Bun
Paté, Omelette, Tart
Paté, Omelette, Bun

Camembert, Salad, Tart
Camembert, Salad, Bun
Camembert, Pasta, Tart
Camembert, Pasta, Bun
Camembert, Omelette, Tart
Camembert, Omelette, Bun

Tree diagrams are particularly useful where you need to make a list of all the objects you're trying to count (in this case, three-course meals).

In Example 1, you didn't have to choose the three courses in the order in which they were to be eaten: for instance, you could just as easily have chosen your main course first, then your starter, and finally your dessert. The tree diagram then looks different (see Figure 2) but the number of possible three-course meals is the same, as you can check by counting the nodes along the bottom row.

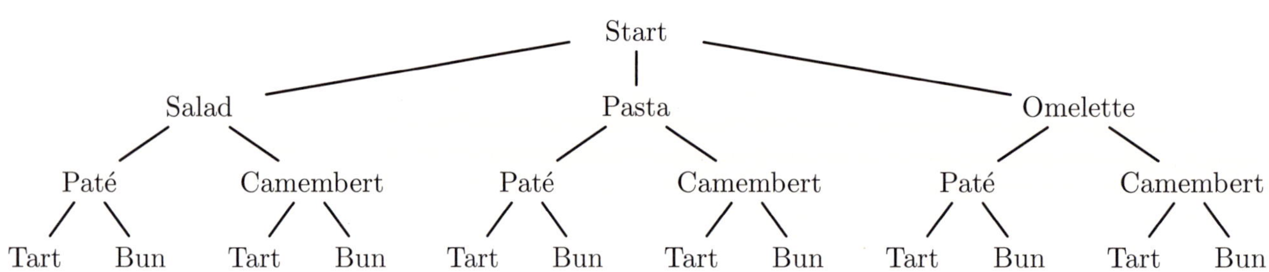

Figure 2 The tree diagram for Example 1 with the courses chosen in a different order

Often, as in Example 1, you'll be asked only to count objects, rather than to list them all. You'll see shortly how you can solve problems like Example 1 without drawing a tree diagram. First, though, here's an activity that involves you drawing another tree diagram.

Activity 1 *Counting the number of vegetarian three-course meals*

Consider again the menu from Example 1. Use a tree diagram to count how many *vegetarian* three-course meals are possible. Make a list of all such meals.

(Vegetarian options are indicated in the menu by (v).)

Notice that, no matter which starter and main course you chose in Example 1 or Activity 1, the same two options were available for dessert.

Thus the bottom part of the tree diagram (shown below) is repeated several times.

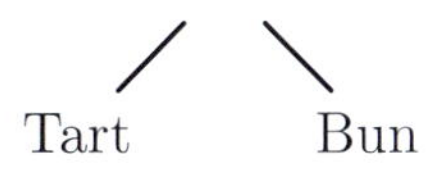

This kind of repetition can make it impractical to draw a tree diagram for a counting problem, unless the total number of possible options is quite small.

Fortunately, you can often solve counting problems without drawing a tree diagram. In Example 1, there are:

- 2 possible starters
- 3 possible main courses
- 2 possible desserts.

The total number of possible three-course meals can be found by multiplying these numbers together, so there are $2 \times 3 \times 2 = 12$ possible three-course meals.

This solution to Example 1 illustrates the following general rule.

The multiplication principle

If you have k successive choices to make, and the ith choice involves choosing from n_i options (for each $i = 1, 2, \ldots, k$), then the total number of ways to make all k choices is

$$n_1 \times n_2 \times \cdots \times n_k.$$

In Example 1, there were three successive choices to make (one for each course), so $k = 3$. The first choice was of a starter, for which there were two possible options, so $n_1 = 2$. Similarly, $n_2 = 3$ is the number of possible main courses and $n_3 = 2$ is the number of possible desserts. By the multiplication principle, the number of possible three-course meals is therefore $n_1 \times n_2 \times n_3 = 2 \times 3 \times 2 = 12$.

The multiplication principle is stated in terms of a counting problem that involves successive choices. It is fairly clear that the problem in Example 1 involves making choices (in this case, the choices of starter, main course and dessert from the menu). Sometimes, however, it is less obvious that a counting problem involves making choices, but you can still use the multiplication principle if you can think of the counting process itself as a succession of choices.

For example, suppose that a menswear shop sells twelve styles of shirts, each of which is available in three colours, and that the manager wants to know the total number of different types of shirts on sale. There is no reference to making choices in the statement of this counting problem. However, you can count the number of types of shirts by first choosing a style option and then choosing a colour option. Since all twelve styles are available in three colours, the number of options for each choice is fixed, and you can use the multiplication principle. There are two successive choices to make (style and colour), so $k = 2$. There are twelve styles, so $n_1 = 12$, and each style is available in three colours, so $n_2 = 3$. By the multiplication principle, the number of different types of shirts on sale is $n_1 \times n_2 = 12 \times 3 = 36$.

Notice that, in this counting problem, it is not essential that each style of shirt is available in the *same* three colours. What is important in applying the multiplication principle is that the *number* of options for a given choice should always be the same, not that the actual options should be identical.

However, you *can't* use the multiplication principle if the number of options for a particular choice changes depending on which options you selected in previous choices. As an example, suppose you want to count the number of possible three-course meals from the menu in Example 1 where *at most one dish contains cheese.* Let's assume that the pasta dish doesn't contain cheese, so that the dishes containing cheese are the baked camembert (a starter) and the mushroom and cheese omelette (a main course). To solve this problem, you need to exclude every three-course meal that includes *both* the camembert *and* the omelette. The tree diagram for this counting problem is shown in Figure 3.

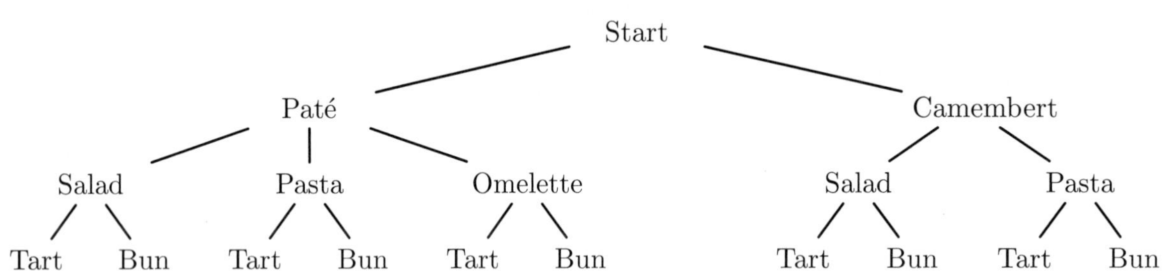

Figure 3 Possible three-course meals with at most one course containing cheese

As you can see from Figure 3, the number of possible main courses is no longer fixed. This is because, if you choose the camembert as a starter, you've already selected a dish containing cheese, so you can't choose the omelette for your main course. As the number of main course options depends on your choice of starter, you can't use the multiplication principle to solve this problem. You can, of course, solve it by using the tree diagram in Figure 3: you can see that there are 10 possible three-course meals with at most one course containing cheese by counting the number of nodes in the bottom row of the diagram.

Here's another example of using the multiplication principle.

Example 2 *Using the multiplication principle*

A businesswoman is being offered a new car by her company. The company has a contract with a particular car manufacturer, which allows her to choose between an estate, a saloon and a hatchback, with each model available in white, red, blue or silver. Petrol and diesel engines are available for all models.

How many ways are there for the businesswoman to choose her new car?

Solution

Identify the important information needed to answer the question.

The businesswoman has to make three successive decisions, to pick the model, colour and engine type of her new car.

There are three types of model (estate, saloon, hatchback), four colours (white, red, blue, silver) and two engine types (petrol, diesel).

To use the multiplication principle, we need to check that the number of options for each of the three decisions is fixed.

We can use the multiplication principle because all four colours and both engine types are available for each model.

Hence there are $3 \times 4 \times 2 = 24$ ways for the businesswoman to choose her new car.

Here are some counting problems where you can try using the multiplication principle. You'll see that, in some of these problems, it would be completely impractical to draw a tree diagram!

Activity 2 *Using the multiplication principle*

(a) A woman is getting ready to take a winter walk. She has two hats, three coats, four pairs of gloves and two pairs of boots. In how many ways can she dress for her walk if she wears hat, coat, gloves and boots?

(b) How many ways are there to answer a ten-question multiple choice test where the first five questions each have four possible answers and the next five questions each have six possible answers?

(c) A password consists of one number, which can be any of the numbers $0, 1, \ldots, 9$, followed by six upper-case letters, each of which can be any of the 26 letters of the alphabet. How many different passwords are possible?

Counting the number of subsets of a set

In the rest of this subsection, you'll see how to use the multiplication principle to work out the number of subsets of a finite set.

Sets were introduced in MST124 Unit 3. The main definitions and notation introduced there are summarised in the box below (you'll also find these in the *Handbook*).

Remember that the objects in a set can be *anything*: numbers, letters of the alphabet, meal choices from a menu, or even other sets. The only condition is that you can't have multiple copies of the same object in a set. So, for example, you can't have two copies of the number 1 in the same set. A collection of objects where multiple copies of the same object are allowed is called a **multiset**.

Sets: notation and definitions

A **set** is a collection of distinct objects.

The notation $x \in A$ means that the object x is in the set A. We say that x is a **member** or an **element** of the set A.

If A and B are any two sets, then

- their **intersection** $A \cap B$ is the set whose members are all the elements that belong to both A and B
- their **union** $A \cup B$ is the set whose members are all the elements that belong to either A or B (or both).

These definitions extend to intersections and unions of more than two sets.

A **subset** of a set A is a set whose elements all belong to A.

The **empty set**, denoted by $\varnothing$, is the set that contains no elements.

The set containing the single element a can be denoted by $\{a\}$. Similarly, the set containing the elements a and b can be denoted by $\{a, b\}$, and so on.

If a set contains a finite number of elements (that is, if the set contains exactly n elements for some non-negative integer n), then we say that the set is a **finite set**. Otherwise, it is an **infinite set**.

As indicated in the box above, when every element of a set A is also an element of a set B, we say that A is a **subset** of B. For example, the set $\{1, 3, 5, 7\}$ is a subset of the set $\{1, 2, 3, 4, 5, 6, 7, 8\}$. Note also that every set is a subset of itself, and that the empty set $\varnothing$ is a subset of every set.

Now suppose that we are given a finite set with n elements. How many subsets does it have? Here's an activity to get you thinking about this question.

Activity 3 *Counting subsets of finite sets*

(a) List all the subsets of the set $\{1,2\}$. Don't forget to include the empty set $\varnothing$ and the set itself! How many subsets are there?

(b) Now list all the subsets of the set $\{1,2,3\}$. How many are there?

For sets with only a few elements, such as the two sets in Activity 3, it's possible to count the number of subsets by listing them all, one by one. Of course, the number of subsets of the set $\{1,2,3\}$ is the same as the number of subsets of the set $\{x,y,z\}$ and the number of subsets of the set $\{A,B,C\}$, and so on: what's important is the *number* of elements in the set, not what kind of elements they are.

Counting the number of subsets of a set by listing them gets harder as the number of elements in the set increases, because it becomes more difficult to be sure that you've found them all! Even for the 4-element set $\{1,2,3,4\}$, it's no easy task to list all the subsets. In fact, there are 16 of them, as follows:

$$\varnothing$$
$$\{1\}\ \{2\}\ \{3\}\ \{4\}$$
$$\{1,2\}\ \{1,3\}\ \{1,4\}\ \{2,3\}\ \{2,4\}\ \{3,4\}$$
$$\{1,2,3\}\ \{1,2,4\}\ \{1,3,4\}\ \{2,3,4\}$$
$$\{1,2,3,4\}$$

If you want to count the number of subsets of a finite set without listing them all, then you can use the multiplication principle, as follows.

Suppose you want to count the subsets of the n-element set $X = \{1,2,\dots,n\}$. The idea is that, to form a subset of X, you look at each element in turn and decide whether or not that element is in the subset. You first choose whether or not the element 1 is in the subset, so there are two options for this first choice. Next, you choose whether or not the element 2 is in the subset: either it's in the subset, or it's not in the subset, so again there are two options. Continuing in this way, for each element of the set X, you have the same two options.

Thus, there are n successive decisions to make, and each decision has the same fixed number of options (two), no matter what choices have already been made. It follows that you can use the multiplication principle, so the number of possible subsets is

$$\underbrace{2 \times 2 \times \cdots \times 2}_{n \text{ times}} = 2^n.$$

This agrees with what you found in Activity 3: a set with two elements has $2^2 = 4$ subsets, and a set with three elements has $2^3 = 8$ subsets.

The number of subsets of an n-element set

A set containing n elements has 2^n subsets, for any non-negative integer n.

The multiplication principle can also be used to count the number of subsets of a set that satisfy certain properties, as the next example shows.

Example 3 *Counting the number of subsets of a set that contain specific elements*

Let $X = \{1, 2, \ldots, n\}$, where n is an integer greater than 1.

(a) How many subsets of X contain the element 1?

(b) How many subsets of X contain at least one of the elements 1 and 2?

Solution

(a) Look at the method used earlier to count the number of subsets of an n-element set. A similar approach will work here.

The element 1 must be in the subset. Each of the remaining $n-1$ elements of X can be chosen either to be included in the subset or to be excluded. Therefore, by the multiplication principle, there are

$$1 \times \underbrace{2 \times 2 \times \cdots \times 2}_{n-1 \text{ times}} = 2^{n-1}$$

subsets of X that contain the element 1.

(b) The elements 1 and 2 are special here, since we want to know how many subsets of X contain at least one of the elements 1 and 2. First write down what these subsets look like.

The subsets of X that we want to count are of the form

$$\{1, \ldots\}, \quad \{2, \ldots\}, \quad \text{or} \quad \{1, 2, \ldots\},$$

where '...' indicates the elements of any subset of $\{3, 4, 5, \ldots, n\}$.

Think about how to choose each such subset by making successive choices.

Split X into two parts, as follows:

$$X = \{1, 2\} \cup \{3, 4, 5, \ldots, n\}.$$

To choose one of the subsets of X that we want to count, we can first choose a subset of $\{1, 2\}$ that contains at least one element, and then choose any subset of $\{3, 4, 5, \ldots, n\}$. The number of options for each of these two choices is unaffected by the option selected for the other choice, so we can use the multiplication principle to calculate the number of subsets that we want to count.

To count the subsets of $\{1, 2\}$ with at least one element, it's easiest just to write them all down.

The subsets of $\{1, 2\}$ containing at least one element are $\{1\}$, $\{2\}$ and $\{1, 2\}$. Thus there are 3 possible options for this choice.

We know that an n-element set has 2^n subsets, so we can immediately write down the number of subsets of an $(n-2)$-element set.

The set $\{3, 4, \ldots, n\}$ contains $n - 2$ elements, so it has 2^{n-2} subsets. Thus there are 2^{n-2} options for this choice.

Now use the multiplication principle.

By the multiplication principle, there are $3 \times 2^{n-2}$ subsets of X that contain at least one of the elements 1 and 2.

You can use ideas similar to those in Example 3 in the next two activities. A good strategy is to begin by finding as large a collection of elements as possible where there is no restriction on which subsets you can pick. This strategy is illustrated by the solution to Example 3(b), where any of the 2^{n-2} subsets of $\{3, 4, 5, \ldots, n\}$ counted towards the final answer.

Activity 4 *Counting subsets that contain specific elements*

(a) Consider the set $\{1, 2, 3, 4\}$.

(i) List all the subsets that do not contain the element 1, but do contain the element 2. How many such subsets are there?

(ii) List all the subsets that contain either the element 1 or the element 2, but not both. How many such subsets are there?

(b) Now let $X = \{1, 2, \ldots, n\}$, where n is an integer greater than 1.

(i) How many subsets of X do not contain the element 1, but do contain the element 2?

(ii) How many subsets of X contain the element 1 or the element 2, but not both?

Activity 5 *Counting subsets of $\{1, 2, \ldots, n\}$ that contain all the odd numbers*

Let $X = \{1, 2, \ldots, n\}$, where n is a positive integer. How many subsets of X contain all the odd numbers from X in each of the following cases?

(a) When n is even. (b) When n is odd.

1.2 The addition principle

In this subsection, you'll learn about a second fundamental principle of counting – the *addition principle*. The addition principle gives you a different way of dealing with a counting problem from those you've already seen with the multiplication principle. You'll see that these two principles are especially powerful when used together.

Let's begin our investigation of the addition principle by revisiting the café menu from Example 1.

Starters
Paté and toast
Baked camembert (v)
Mains
Chicken salad
Penne pasta with tomato and basil sauce (v)
Mushroom and cheese omelette (v)
Desserts
Apple tart (v)
Iced Chelsea bun (v)

Consider the following question:

> How many different meals are possible if a meal must consist of three courses, or a starter and a main course, or a main course and a dessert?

You know from Example 1 that there are 12 possible three-course meals. In the next activity, you'll count the other two types of meals.

Activity 6 *Counting the number of two-course meals*

Use the multiplication principle to count the number of meals consisting of each of the following two courses.

(a) A starter and a main course. (b) A main course and a dessert.

Now let's return to the question posed before Activity 6. We need a way to combine the 12 three-course meals with the 6 two-course meals consisting of a starter and a main course, and the 6 two-course meals consisting of a main course and a dessert. The multiplication principle is of no help here: $12 \times 6 \times 6 = 432$ is the number of ways of ordering a three-course meal *and* a starter plus a main course *and* a main course plus a dessert. What we are looking for is the number of meals consisting of three courses *or* a starter and a main course *or* a main course and a dessert.

To work this out, one approach is to first decide between the three types of meals, and then to choose the courses that will make up the meal. This can be illustrated using a tree diagram, as shown in Figure 4. To save space, we have used some abbreviations: S = salad, P = pasta, O = omelette, T = tart and B = bun.

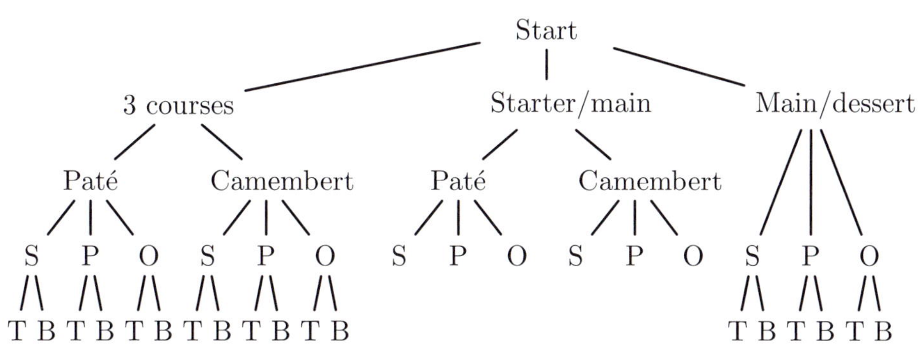

Figure 4 A tree diagram counting the number of meals consisting of three courses, or a starter and a main, or a main and a dessert

Notice that the tree diagram in Figure 4 is made up of three smaller tree diagrams joined together, with each of the smaller tree diagrams corresponding to one of the three meal types. The total number of two- or three-course meals is equal to the number of nodes along the bottom of the tree diagram, and this is equal to the sum of the numbers of nodes at the bottom of each of the three smaller tree diagrams. In other words, we can write

$$\begin{aligned}\text{number of 2- or 3-course meals} &= \text{number of 3-course meals}\\ &\quad+\text{number of starter/main meals}\\ &\quad+\text{number of main/dessert meals.}\end{aligned}$$

From the solutions to Example 1 and Activity 6, this means that

$$\text{number of 2- or 3-course meals} = 12 + 6 + 6 = 24.$$

When approaching a counting problem such as this one, it's useful to think of the collection of objects you're trying to count as a *set*. The counting problem is then the same as finding the size of this set (that is, the number of elements in the set). The **size** of a set S is usually written as $|S|$.

For instance, the question we've just answered can be rephrased to ask for the size of the set S of all possible 2- and 3-course meals that include a main course. The solution we found above divided this set into three subsets S_1, S_2 and S_3, as follows:

S_1 = the subset containing all 3-course meals
S_2 = the subset containing all starter/main meals
S_3 = the subset containing all main/dessert meals.

From the point of view of counting the number of elements in S, this division into subsets has two important properties:

- S is equal to the union of the three subsets, that is,

  $$S = S_1 \cup S_2 \cup S_3,$$

  so every element of S belongs to one of the subsets.
- No element of S belongs to more than one of the subsets. That is, the intersections between any two of S_1, S_2 and S_3 contain no elements:

  $$S_1 \cap S_2 = \varnothing, \quad S_1 \cap S_3 = \varnothing \quad \text{and} \quad S_2 \cap S_3 = \varnothing.$$

  When a collection of sets has the property that the intersection of any two sets in the collection is empty, the sets in the collection are said to be **pairwise disjoint sets**. (Two sets whose intersection is empty are said to be **disjoint**.)

Activity 7 *Learning about pairwise disjoint sets*

For each of the following collections of sets, say whether or not the sets in the collection are pairwise disjoint.

(a) $\{2, 4, 6\}$ and $\{1, 3, 5\}$

(b) $\{1, 3\}$, $\{2, 4\}$ and $\{1, 2\}$

(c) {pasta, camembert, tart}, {bun, salad}, and {paté, omelette}

(d) {paté, omelette}, {camembert, pasta} and {paté, salad}

Now let's return to our discussion about two- and three-course meals. From the solutions to Example 1 and Activity 6, we know that

$$|S_1| = 12, \ |S_2| = 6 \text{ and } |S_3| = 6.$$

We've also seen that the total number $|S|$ of two- or three-course meals is given by

$$|S| = |S_1| + |S_2| + |S_3| = 12 + 6 + 6 = 24.$$

Therefore, we can count the number of elements in the set S by counting the numbers of elements in each subset, and adding these numbers together.

This illustrates the following general rule, which applies whenever you can divide a set into a finite number of pairwise disjoint subsets whose union is the whole set.

The addition principle

If a set S can be divided into a collection of k pairwise disjoint subsets $S_1, S_2, \ldots, S_k$ whose union is S, then

$$|S| = |S_1| + |S_2| + \cdots + |S_k|.$$

The addition principle is useful in solving a wide range of counting problems, especially when used together with the multiplication principle. You've already seen an example of this in the discussion about two- and three-course meals.

As another example, let's revisit the problem of counting the number of possible three-course meals from the menu in Example 1 where at most one dish contains cheese (we previously looked at this on page 10). You'll remember that you couldn't solve this problem using the multiplication principle, because the number of options for the main course depends on your choice of starter – if you choose the starter containing cheese (baked camembert), then you can't select the omelette for your main course because you've already chosen a cheese course.

However, you *can* solve this problem by using the addition principle together with the multiplication principle. Let's use S to denote the set of all possible three-course meals where at most one dish contains cheese. You can split S into the following two disjoint subsets:

S_1 = meals in S where the starter contains cheese

S_2 = meals in S where the starter does not contain cheese.

Now let's work out the size of each of these subsets. For a meal in S_1, there is only one option for the starter (camembert), two options for the main course (pasta or salad) and two options for dessert (tart or bun). The number of options is fixed for each choice so we can use the multiplication principle, and we find that

$$|S_1| = 1 \times 2 \times 2 = 4.$$

Similarly, for a meal in S_2, there is only one option for the starter (paté), three options for the main course (omelette, pasta or salad) and two options for dessert (tart or bun). The number of options is fixed for each choice, so again we can use the multiplication principle, which gives

$$|S_2| = 1 \times 3 \times 2 = 6.$$

Finally, since S_1 and S_2 are disjoint and $S = S_1 \cup S_2$, we can use the addition principle to work out the size of S:

$$|S| = |S_1| + |S_2| = 4 + 6 = 10.$$

This agrees with the answer we found previously by using a tree diagram.

This example illustrates the general point that, when you can't solve a counting problem by using the multiplication principle because the number of options for a certain choice depends on the choices already made, you may be able to divide up the set you're trying to count into disjoint subsets, and then solve the problem by using the addition principle and the multiplication principle together.

Here's a slightly more complicated example of using these two principles in combination. It's about the **decimal representation** of integers, which means the usual way we write down integers. For example, '731' is the decimal representation for the integer that has 7 hundreds, 3 tens and 1 unit.

Example 4 *Using the addition principle and the multiplication principle together*

How many positive integers less than 1000 do not contain the digit 1 in their decimal representations?

Solution

Express the problem in terms of sets.

The set to be counted is the set of all positive integers less than 1000 that do not contain the digit 1 in their decimal representations. Call this set S.

Think about what the elements of S look like and hence try to split S into pairwise disjoint subsets whose elements are easier to count. For example, the number 528 is in S because it does not contain a 1 in its decimal representation. It is formed by choosing each of the three digits 5, 2 and 8 in turn, ensuring each time that 1 is not chosen. On the other hand, the number 74 is also in S. This is formed by choosing just two digits. This suggests dividing S into three subsets, containing the 1-, 2- and 3-digit numbers from S respectively, and counting them separately.

Divide the problem into cases, depending on how many digits there are in an element of S. Let

S_1 = the subset consisting of all 1-digit numbers in S

S_2 = the subset consisting of all 2-digit numbers in S

S_3 = the subset consisting of all 3-digit numbers in S.

Check that S is equal to the union of the subsets, and that the subsets are pairwise disjoint. This means that we can use the addition principle.

Every number in S clearly has $1, 2$ or 3 digits, and so lies in exactly one of S_1, S_2 or S_3, which are therefore pairwise disjoint. Hence it follows from the addition principle that

$$|S| = |S_1| + |S_2| + |S_3|.$$

To determine the size of S_1, we can write down all the elements it contains. Note that 0 is excluded, since S contains only positive integers.

Now $S_1 = \{2, 3, 4, 5, 6, 7, 8, 9\}$, so $|S_1| = 8$.

For two-digit numbers, choose each of the two digits in turn and use the multiplication principle. Think about the possible options for each choice of digit:

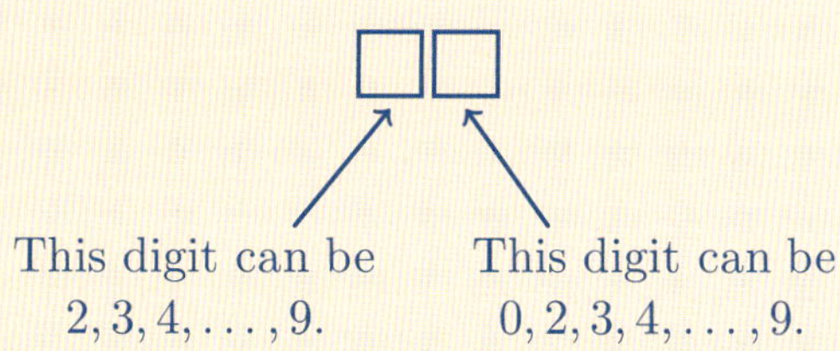

Consider a number in S_2. The tens digit of this number cannot be 0 or 1, so it must be one of the eight numbers $2, 3, 4, \ldots, 9$. The units digit can be 0, or one of $2, 3, 4, \ldots, 9$, so there are nine options for this choice. Each of these digits is chosen separately, and the number of options for each choice is fixed. Hence, by the multiplication principle,

$$|S_2| = 8 \times 9 = 72.$$

Count three-digit numbers in a similar way. Again, think about the possible options for each digit:

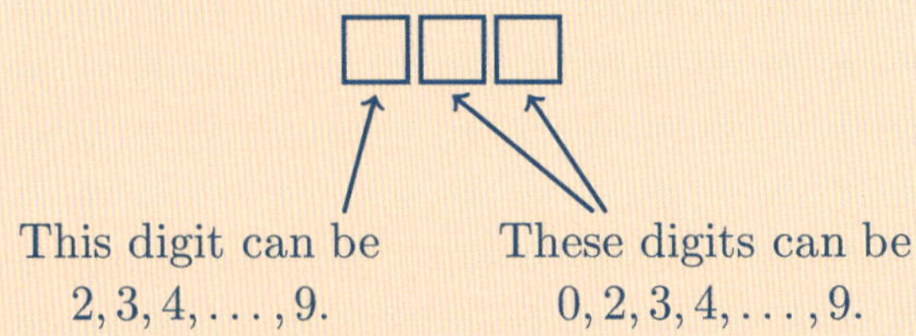

Now consider a number in S_3. There are 8 options for the hundreds digit, and 9 options each for the tens and units digits. Hence, by the multiplication principle,

$$|S_3| = 8 \times 9 \times 9 = 648.$$

Now recombine the three cases using the addition principle.

Therefore it follows by the addition principle that the number of positive integers less than 1000 that do not contain a 1 in their decimal representations is

$$8 + 72 + 648 = 728.$$

There is, in fact, another way to solve the problem in Example 4, without using the addition principle. In this approach, you treat *every* number less than 1000 as consisting of 3 digits, by adding leading 0s. For example, you can write the number 43 as 043, and the number 7 as 007. The following diagram illustrates the options for each of the three digits: there are 9 possible options for each.

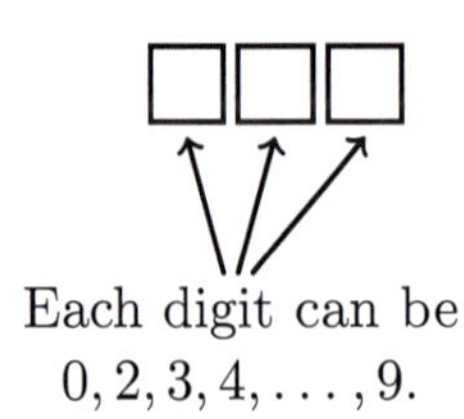

Since there are three digits to choose, and 9 options for each digit, the multiplication principle tells us that there are $9 \times 9 \times 9 = 9^3 = 729$ three-digit numbers that do not contain a 1 in their decimal representations. However, something has gone wrong – we have counted one more element this way than we did in the solution to Example 4!

The problem here is that, in the diagram above, it is possible to choose the hundreds digit to be 0, the tens digit to be 0, and also the units digit to be 0. That is, we have counted the number 0 (as '000') in our solution, but the question asked only for positive integers. Hence we need to remove '000' from our count in the second method, and we then find that the number of positive integers less than 1000 that do not contain a 1 in their decimal representations is indeed $729 - 1 = 728$, as before.

This alternative approach to solving Example 4 demonstrates two things. First, you need to be careful to count only those elements that are in the set! Second, it is quite common for there to be more than one way to solve a counting problem, arising from different counting strategies. In some cases, you'll find that one counting strategy leads to a much shorter solution than another.

Activity 8 *Using the addition principle and the multiplication principle together*

(a) A bookshelf contains five Spanish books, six French books and eight Italian books. How many ways are there of picking two books in different languages?

(b) A storage cupboard at a factory can be opened by typing the correct numerical access code into a keypad on the door. The access code can be four, five or six digits long, and each digit is one of the numbers $0, 1, \dots, 9$. How many possible access codes are there?

(c) How many positive integers less than 1000 do not contain any odd digits in their decimal representations?

1.3 The subtraction principle

Sometimes, in order to count the number of elements in a set, it's easier to first count the elements in a bigger set, then count the elements that you don't want, and subtract the second number from the first.

For example, the alternative solution to Example 4 on page 22 took exactly this approach. We wanted to count the number of positive integers less than 1000 that do not contain the digit 1. In order to do this, we first worked out that there are $9^3 = 729$ numbers between 0 and 999 (inclusive) that do not contain the digit 1. However, this is a larger set than we wanted, because it included the number 0, which is not a positive integer. Thus, we subtracted the number of elements that we didn't want (in this case, just one) and concluded that there are $729 - 1 = 728$ numbers between 1 and 999 that do not contain the digit 1.

This illustrates our third fundamental principle of counting, the *subtraction principle*. To state this principle in terms of sets, we first introduce another definition.

If a set S is a subset of a set U, then the set of all elements of U that are *not* elements of S is called the **complement** of S in U, and is written $\overline{S}$.

For example, the set $\{2, 4, 8\}$ is a subset of the set $\{2, 4, 6, 8, 10\}$, and its complement in that set is $\{6, 10\}$.

The letter U is used for the larger set because it is sometimes referred to as a **universal set**. In some texts, you might see the notation S^c rather than $\overline{S}$ used to mean the complement of S in the larger set U.

The subtraction principle shows how the size of a set S is related to the sizes of U and of $\overline{S}$.

The subtraction principle

If the set S is a subset of the finite set U, then

$$|S| = |U| - |\overline{S}|.$$

The skill in using the subtraction principle to solve a problem that involves counting the number of elements in a set S is to find a suitable larger set U in such a way that it's easier to count the elements of both U and $\overline{S}$ than it is to count the elements of S directly.

We can write the alternative solution to Example 4 in terms of the subtraction principle as follows. We want to find the size of the set

$$S = \text{set of all positive integers less than 1000 not containing a 1.}$$

Define

$$U = \text{set of all non-negative integers less than 1000 not containing a 1.}$$

There is only one element in U that is not in S, namely 0, so the complement of S in U is

$$\overline{S} = \{0\}.$$

After establishing that U contains $9^3 = 729$ elements, the subtraction principle can be applied to give

$$|S| = |U| - |\overline{S}| = 729 - 1 = 728.$$

In the next example, we count the number of positive integers less than 1000 with *at least one* 1 in their decimal representations.

Example 5 *Using the subtraction principle*

How many positive integers less than 1000 have at least one 1 in their decimal representations?

Solution

Express the problem in terms of sets.

We need to count the set

S = set of all positive integers less than 1000 containing at least one 1.

You *could* count the elements in S directly, by dividing up S according to how many 1s each element contains: exactly one 1, exactly two 1s, or exactly three 1s. However, counting each of these subsets is still going to be complicated, because you need to know which positions (hundreds, tens, or units) the 1s are in.

Instead, you can make use of the solution to Example 4, which tells you how many positive integers less than 1000 do not contain a 1 in their decimal representations. These are exactly the numbers from $\{1, 2, 3, \ldots, 999\}$ that we *don't* want. So, if U is the set of all integers from 1 to 999, you can use the subtraction principle to find $|S|$.

Let $U = \{1, 2, \ldots, 999\}$. Note that $|U| = 999$, and that S is a subset of U. Since every number in U either contains at least one 1, or contains no 1s, we conclude that the complement of S in U is the set

$\overline{S}$ = set of all positive integers less than 1000 not containing a 1.

By the solution to Example 4, we know that $|\overline{S}| = 728$. Therefore, by the subtraction principle,

$$|S| = |U| - |\overline{S}| = 999 - 728 = 271.$$

Hence there are 271 positive integers less than 1000 with at least one 1 in their decimal representations.

Example 5 is an instance of a common situation where the subtraction principle can be used to make the process of counting easier. The phrase 'at least one' is a short way of saying 'one, or two, or three, or …'. So, to count objects with at least one of 'something' directly, you would first have to count the numbers of objects with one, and then with two, and then with three of the 'something', and so on, and finally use the addition principle to combine these numbers to get the total. Instead, it is often much easier to use the subtraction principle, by first counting the objects that have none of the 'something', and then subtracting this number from the total number of objects.

Here are some counting problems for you to try. Note that not all parts of the activity require you to use the subtraction principle.

Activity 9 *Using the subtraction principle*

(a) How many positive integers less than 1000 contain at least one odd digit in their decimal representations? (Hint: use your answer to Activity 8(c)).

(b) Four letters are selected in turn, each of which can be any of the 26 upper-case letters $A, B, C, \dots, Z$. The selected letters are written one after another to form a 'word' – for example, $ZRPI$ and $AHHD$ are two possible words.

  (i) How many different words are possible?

  (ii) How many of these contain no vowels (the vowels are the letters A, E, I, O and U)?

  (iii) How many contain at least one vowel?

(c) A fruit seller has 6 apples, 5 oranges and 3 pears, and is preparing a basket of fruit for a customer.

  (i) Including the basket containing no fruit, how many different baskets of fruit are possible?

  (ii) How many baskets of fruit are possible if the basket must contain at least one piece of fruit?

  (iii) How many baskets of fruit are possible if the basket must contain at least two pieces of fruit?

1.4 Choosing strategies for solving counting problems

You've now met three fundamental principles of counting – the multiplication principle, the addition principle and the subtraction principle – and seen how they can be used, individually and together, to solve a variety of counting problems.

Of course, you don't usually know in advance which of these principles to apply to a particular problem. You'll need to think carefully about the problem and about the nature of the set you're trying to count, and then decide on a strategy for using the counting principles to solve the problem. You may also be able to find more than one strategy that works.

Because of the huge range of counting problems, it's not possible to give step-by-step instructions on how to choose a counting strategy. However, the steps and suggestions in the following box may help in each case.

Choosing a strategy for solving a counting problem

The following steps may help.

1. Express the problem in terms of counting elements of a set S.
2. Pick some element from S, and try to identify a sequence of simple decisions that together are equivalent to choosing this element. It may help to sketch part of a tree diagram for the problem.
3. Look at the sequence of decisions that you identified in step 2. Ask yourself what other options could be selected at each decision, and what other elements of S can be chosen in this way.
4. Repeat steps 2 and 3 until you have a good understanding of how all the elements of S can be chosen. Each time you pick a new element, try to construct a sequence of decisions that is similar to the sequences of decisions that you have already found.
5. Using your sequence(s) of decisions, try to find ways to use the counting principles to count the total number of elements of S.
   - Use the multiplication principle when you have a sequence of decisions where the number of options for each decision is not affected by decisions already made.
   - It may help to divide the problem into a few subproblems, by splitting S into a number of pairwise disjoint subsets. You may then be able to use the multiplication principle to count the number of elements in each subset, and use the addition principle to find the total number of elements in S.
   - In particular, when you have a decision that affects the number of options for subsequent decisions, you may find that you can use the addition principle together with the multiplication principle in the way described above.
   - Think about whether S is a subset of a larger set U, where both U and the complement $\overline{S}$ of S in U are easier to count than S. If so, use the subtraction principle.
   - In particular, the subtraction principle is often useful for problems that contain phrases such as 'at least one', or 'one or more'.

Try using the ideas in the box above to help you solve the following counting problems.

Activity 10 *Choosing strategies to solve counting problems*

(a) How many positive integers are there whose decimal representations consist of two digits, with no digits repeated?

(b) Let n be a positive integer, and suppose that n letters are selected in turn, each of which can be any of the 26 upper-case letters $A, B, C, \ldots, Z$. The selected letters are written one after another to form a 'word' of length n.

A *palindrome* is a word that reads the same both forwards and backwards – for example, $GQHQG$ is a palindrome of length 5. How many palindromes are there of length n?

(Hint: consider separately the cases where n is even and n is odd).

(c) How many positive integers are there whose decimal representations consist of two digits, and whose digits are in decreasing order – that is, the 'units' digit is less than the 'tens' digit?

(d) A safety deposit box in a hotel room has a four-character access code that must be entered to open or close the box. Each character in the access code can be any of the numbers $0, 1, 2, \ldots, 9$, or any of the letters $A, B, C, \ldots, Z$, but at most one of the first two characters can be a letter. How many possible access codes are there?

There will be more opportunities for you to practise using these fundamental principles of counting in the next section, where you'll learn about sequences, combinations and permutations.

2 Sequences, permutations and combinations

Consider the following problem.

> How many ways are there to choose k numbers from the set $\{1, 2, 3, \ldots, n\}$, where k and n are positive integers?

To solve this problem, you first need more information. There are two points that are unclear and need to be resolved:

1. Is the order in which you pick the k numbers important?

   For example, if you are picking 2 numbers from the set $\{1, 2, 3, 4\}$, and you choose '1, then 2', is this different from choosing '2, then 1'?
2. Are repetitions allowed? That is, can you pick the same number more than once?

   So, with the same example, can you choose '1, then 1'?

Each of these questions has two possible answers ('yes' or 'no'), so (by the multiplication principle!) there are four ways of interpreting the original problem.

Suppose first that the order in which the numbers are chosen is important. In this case, you are choosing what is called an **arrangement**. If repetitions are not allowed, then the arrangement is called a **permutation**. If repetitions are allowed, then the arrangement is called a **sequence**.

If, on the other hand, the order in which the numbers are chosen is not important, then you are choosing what is called a **selection**. If repetitions are not allowed, then the selection is called a **combination**. If repetitions are allowed, then the selection is called a **multiset**.

Table 1 summarises the four possible interpretations of the original problem, and gives the name for the collection of objects being counted in each case. Notice that, when thought of in terms of sets, a combination is just a subset.

Table 1 The four different ways of choosing k objects from n objects

	Repetitions not allowed	Repetitions allowed
Order important (an arrangement)	Permutation	Sequence
Order not important (a selection)	Combination	Multiset

In this section, you'll learn about counting sequences, permutations and combinations. We will not consider counting multisets in this module. (Except briefly in the next example!)

Example 6 *Understanding sequences, permutations, combinations and multisets*

Let $S = \{A, B, C\}$. List all of the 2-element sequences, permutations, combinations and multisets that can be chosen from elements of S. How many are there of each?

Solution

Consider each type in turn. Start by listing the *sequences*, where the order matters and repetition is allowed.

To ensure you've listed all the elements, try to find a systematic way to write them down. A good way when dealing with letters is to list them in alphabetical order. So list all the sequences beginning with A first, then those beginning with B, and so on.

The 2-element sequences are

$$AA, AB, AC, BA, BB, BC, CA, CB, CC,$$

so there are 9 of them.

Next list the *permutations*, where the order matters but repetition is not allowed. This means that AA, BB and CC are not permutations, but all the other sequences listed above are.

The 2-element permutations are

$$AB, AC, BA, BC, CA, CB,$$

so there are 6 of them.

Now list the *combinations*, where the order does not matter and repetitions are not allowed. Note that the permutation AB and the permutation BA both correspond to the same combination. Similarly, AC and CA correspond to the same combination, and so do BC and CB.

There are three 2-element combinations, namely AB, AC and BC.

Finally, list the *multisets*, where the order does not matter and repetitions are allowed. In this case, the multisets are the three combinations listed above, together with AA, BB and CC.

The 2-element multisets are

$$AA, AB, AC, BB, BC, CC,$$

so there are 6 of them.

2.1 Sequences

You can use the multiplication principle to count the number of k-element sequences that can be chosen from n objects.

Activity 11 *Counting sequences*

How many sequences of the upper-case letters $A, B, C, \ldots, Z$ are there, for each of the following lengths of sequences?

(a) 2-letter sequences.

(b) 3-letter sequences.

(c) k-letter sequences, for some positive integer k.

Now suppose you're asked to pick a k-element sequence from a collection of n objects. You can use the same approach as in Activity 11, where you were counting sequences of letters. You can pick each of the k elements of the sequence in turn, and each element can be any of the n objects because repetitions are allowed. Thus there are

n choices for the first element of the sequence,

n choices for the second element of the sequence,

$\vdots$

n choices for the kth element of the sequence.

Hence, by the multiplication principle, the number of k-element sequences of n objects is

$$\underbrace{n \times n \times \cdots \times n}_{k \text{ times}} = n^k.$$

Notice that, if we take the view that there is only one way to choose a 0-element sequence from any set, then this formula also holds for $k = 0$, since $n^0 = 1$ for any value of n.

The number of k-element sequences of n objects

Let n be a positive integer and k a non-negative integer.

Then there are n^k different k-element sequences of n objects.

2.2 Permutations

Recall from Table 1 that a **permutation** is an arrangement of objects in a particular order, with no repetitions. For example,

$$CAB$$

is a permutation of the letters A, B and C, but

$$CCA$$

is not a permutation, because the letter C occurs twice.

Activity 12 *Listing the permutations of three letters*

There are six three-letter permutations of the letters A, B and C. Write them all down.

The permutations you listed in Activity 12 are the 3-element permutations of the three letters A, B and C. In Example 6, you saw that there are six 2-element permutations chosen from the letters in the set $\{A, B, C\}$, namely

$$AB, AC, BA, BC, CA, CB.$$

Our next aim is to find a formula to count the number of k-element permutations of n objects, for any k and n (just as we did above for sequences). These permutations are sometimes called **permutations of n objects taken k at a time**.

Obviously, if $k > n$, then there are no permutations: you cannot choose more than n items from an n-element set without picking one of them at least twice!

Let's begin to explore the number of permutations when $k \leq n$ by looking at a specific example. Suppose you wish to count the number of permutations of the 26 upper-case letters of the alphabet taken 3 at a time. In Activity 11, you found that there are $26^3 = 17\,576$ sequences of three letters. Not all of these sequences are permutations (because some of them will contain repeated letters), but it's clear that we can't count the permutations by listing them all – there are far too many!

Instead, let's look at each position of the permutation in turn. For the first position of the permutation, there are 26 choices, because there are no constraints yet.

For the second position, we can pick any of the 26 letters of the alphabet, except for the one that was picked for the first position. Therefore, there are 25 choices for this position.

Finally, for the third position, by the same reasoning there are 24 choices: any letter can be chosen, except for the two letters that have already been selected.

Clearly, the range of letters available for the second and third positions of the permutation depend on which letters have already been chosen for earlier positions. However, the *numbers* of letters available for the second and third positions are always the same (25 and 24 respectively), and this is all that is needed to allow you to use the multiplication principle. Hence there are

$$26 \times 25 \times 24 = 15\,600$$

permutations of the 26 letters of the alphabet taken 3 at a time.

Now let's return to the general question: the number of permutations of n objects taken k at a time, for $k \leq n$. This is an important number in mathematics, and it has its own notation. The number of permutations of n objects taken k at a time is denoted by the symbol ${}^nP_k$, which is read as 'n p k'.

To find ${}^nP_k$, let's proceed as before and look in turn at each of the k positions of the permutation. There are

$$\begin{aligned} n &\text{ options for the 1st position,} \\ n-1 &\text{ options for the 2nd position,} \\ n-2 &\text{ options for the 3rd position,} \\ &\vdots \\ n-(k-1) &\text{ options for the } k\text{th position.} \end{aligned}$$

Note that the number of options at each step is fixed, which means that we can apply the multiplication principle. Thus, the number of permutations of n objects taken k at a time is

$${}^nP_k = n \times (n-1) \times \cdots \times (n-k+1).$$

Remember that the product $n \times (n-1) \times \cdots \times 2 \times 1$ of the first n positive integers is denoted by the symbol $n!$ and is called the **factorial** of n. (The notation $n!$ is read as 'n factorial' or 'factorial n'.) We can use this fact to express ${}^nP_k$ more neatly, as follows.

$$\begin{aligned} {}^nP_k &= n(n-1)\cdots(n-k+1) \\ &= \frac{n(n-1)\cdots(n-k+1)(n-k)!}{(n-k)!} \\ &= \frac{n!}{(n-k)!}. \end{aligned}$$

If we take the view that there is only one way to choose a 0-element permutation from any set (as we did for 0-element sequences), then this formula holds for $k = 0$, since

$${}^nP_0 = \frac{n!}{(n-0)!} = \frac{n!}{n!} = 1.$$

The number of permutations of n objects taken k at a time

Let n be a positive integer and k a non-negative integer less than or equal to n. Then

$$\begin{aligned} {}^nP_k &= n(n-1)\cdots(n-k+1) \qquad (1)\\ &= \frac{n!}{(n-k)!}. \qquad (2)\end{aligned}$$

Although formula (2) is neater, you'll usually find that formula (1) is more convenient for calculating values of ${}^nP_k$. It is important to remember that, in formula (1), the multiplication goes down to $n-k+1$, and *not* to $n-k$.

The number of permutations of the full set of n objects is given by ${}^nP_n$. Substituting $k=n$ into equation (1) gives

$${}^nP_n = n(n-1)\cdots(n-n+1) = n!.$$

Example 7 *Counting permutations*

How many five-letter permutations can be made from the letters A, B, C, D, E, F, G, H?

Solution

The question is asking for the number of permutations of 8 letters taken 5 at a time.

There are eight letters to choose from, and we need permutations containing 5 of these. Thus $n=8$ and $k=5$, and on substituting these values in formula (1) we obtain

$${}^8P_5 = 8\times 7\times 6\times 5\times 4 = 6720.$$

Activity 13 *Counting ways to award gold, silver and bronze medals*

A university is holding its annual athletics competition. In the 1500 metre race, gold, silver and bronze medals will be awarded respectively to the first, second and third competitors to cross the finish line.

If there are 16 competitors taking part in the race, how many ways are there to award the medals?

2.3 Combinations

Recall from Table 1 that a **combination** is a selection of k objects from a collection of n objects, in which the order does not matter and repetitions are not allowed. In Example 6, you saw that there are three 2-letter combinations of letters taken from the three letters A, B, and C, namely:

$$AB, \quad AC, \quad BC.$$

The combinations of k objects from a set of n objects are really just the k-element subsets of the set of n objects, though they are usually written without the curly brackets and commas. For example, the 2-element subsets of $\{A, B, C\}$ are

$$\{A, B\}, \quad \{A, C\}, \quad \{B, C\}.$$

Formally, a selection of k different objects from a collection of n objects, in which the order does not matter, is called a **combination of n objects taken k at a time**. Our next aim is to count how many such combinations there are.

Let's begin by considering a specific example. Suppose you wish to count the number of combinations of the 26 upper-case letters taken 3 at a time. This is the same as counting the number of 3-element subsets of $\{A, B, C, \ldots, Z\}$. So

$$\{A, B, C\}, \quad \{F, M, T\}, \quad \{Q, R, Z\}$$

are examples of the subsets that need to be counted.

Let's look at the subset $\{A, B, C\}$. In Activity 12, you found that there are six permutations of these letters, as follows:

$$\begin{array}{lll} ABC, & BAC, & CAB, \\ ACB, & BCA, & CBA. \end{array}$$

In fact, for *any* three-letter subset of the alphabet, there will be ${}^{3}P_{3} = 6$ permutations of the letters. This means that for every three-element subset, or equivalently, for every combination of 3 elements, we can find 6 different permutations.

Earlier, you learned that there are ${}^{26}P_{3} = 15\,600$ permutations of the 26 letters of the alphabet, taken 3 at a time. Since there are six permutations for every combination, there must be

$$\frac{15\,600}{6} = 2600$$

combinations of the 26 letters taken 3 at a time.

To find a general formula for the number of combinations of n objects taken k at a time, start with the number ${}^nP_k$, which is the number of permutations of n objects taken k at a time. View each combination as a subset containing k elements, and consider one particular subset. Using the elements in this subset, you can form ${}^kP_k = k!$ corresponding permutations.

Consequently, for every combination that we need to count, there are $k!$ permutations. So, since there are ${}^nP_k$ permutations, there must be

$$\frac{{}^nP_k}{k!}$$

combinations. Now

$$\begin{aligned}\frac{{}^nP_k}{k!} &= \frac{n(n-1)\cdots(n-k+1)}{k!}\\ &= \frac{n(n-1)\cdots(n-k+1)\times(n-k)!}{k!(n-k)!}\\ &= \frac{n!}{(n-k)!\,k!}.\end{aligned}$$

You may recognise this expression. It's the same as the expression for the kth coefficient in row n of Pascal's triangle. These coefficients are called *binomial coefficients*, and they were covered in MST124 Unit 10.

In MST124, we used the symbol ${}^nC_k$ (pronounced 'n c k' or 'n choose k') for these quantities, and we'll continue to use the same notation here.

The number of combinations of n objects taken k at a time

Let n be a positive integer and k a non-negative integer less than or equal to n. Then

$$\begin{aligned}{}^nC_k = \frac{{}^nP_k}{k!} &= \frac{n(n-1)\cdots(n-k+1)}{k!} \qquad (3)\\ &= \frac{n!}{(n-k)!\,k!} \qquad (4)\end{aligned}$$

Formula (3) is usually the most convenient to use for practical calculations.

Example 8 *Counting the number of ways to form a subcommittee*

In how many ways can a subcommittee of 4 be selected from a committee of 10 people? (Note that, in selecting a subcommitee, the order of the selection does not matter.)

Solution

Since the order of selection of members of the subcommittees does not matter, and since the members of the subcommittee must be 4 distinct people (that is, repetitions are not allowed), we need to count the number of combinations of 10 people taken 4 at a time.

The number of possible subcommittees is equal to the number of combinations of 10 people taken 4 at a time, which is

$$^{10}C_4 = \frac{10 \times 9 \times 8 \times 7}{4 \times 3 \times 2 \times 1} = 210.$$

Activity 14 *Counting meals from a tapas menu*

In a tapas bar, diners choose several small dishes to be brought to the table all at the same time. The current menu is shown below.

Stuffed red peppers
Patatas bravas
Calamares
Tomato and goat's cheese salad
Chorizo
Spanish meatballs 'Albondigas'

How many meals are possible, if a customer has to choose 3 different dishes?

In the next activity, you need to decide in each case whether you should count sequences, permutations or combinations.

Activity 15 *Selecting students from a class in different scenarios*

There are 15 students in a class. How many different possibilities are there for each of the following?

(a) A team of six of the students.

(b) A prize list awarding first, second, third, fourth and fifth prizes to five of the students.

(c) A list showing the top student in each of three exams taken by the whole class.

It's often helpful to use permutations and combinations as part of strategies for solving counting problems. Here's an example.

Example 9 *Using combinations in a counting strategy*

A mathematics class consists of 7 mathematics students, 6 science students and 4 computer science students. How many ways are there to choose a team of six students to meet a visitor, if the team must consist of two of each type of student?

Solution

Find a sequence of decisions that together are equivalent to choosing a particular team.

Each team can be chosen by first choosing the two mathematics students, then the two science students and finally the two computer science students.

The number of options for each of these three decisions is not affected by decisions already made, so the multiplication principle can be used. When the students of a particular type are chosen, the order of choosing does not matter, and repetitions are not allowed.

The number of ways to choose the mathematics students is ${}^7C_2 = 21$.

The number of ways to choose the science students is ${}^6C_2 = 15$.

The number of ways to choose the computer science students is ${}^4C_2 = 6$.

Hence, by the multiplication principle, the total number of ways to choose the team is $21 \times 15 \times 6 = 1890$.

Here are some counting problems for you to try to solve by using permutations or combinations as part of counting strategies. You might find it helpful to look back at the suggestions for choosing counting strategies that you met in Subsection 1.4.

Activity 16 *Using permutations and combinations in counting strategies*

(a) The marketing department in a company consists of four junior employees and three senior employees. It has to choose a team of four of these employees to make a foreign visit. If there must be two junior employees and two senior employees in the team, how many ways are there to choose the team?

(b) A class of children contains 14 boys and 12 girls. How many ways are there to choose a team of six children from the class if it must contain at least two boys and at least two girls?

(c) Consider the four-digit integers that can be made by using the digits 1, 2, 3, 4, 5 and 6 at most once each.

(i) How many such integers are there altogether?

(ii) How many are larger than 6000?

(iii) How many are larger than 5000?

(iv) How many are smaller than 5000?

2.4 Connections with probability

So far, you've been counting the number of ways to *choose* objects that satisfy specified rules. In this subsection, you'll explore how to use the same methods to calculate the *chances* of something happening. In other words, you'll learn about some connections between solving counting problems and solving problems in probability.

In the study of probability, an **outcome** is a possible result of some experiment or process. For example, if you toss a coin, there are two possible outcomes – heads (H) or tails (T). If you roll a normal six-sided die, there are six possible outcomes – 1, 2, 3, 4, 5 or 6. Since the number of possible outcomes is fixed in each case, it follows from the multiplication principle that if you toss a coin *and* roll a die, then there are $2 \times 6 = 12$ possible outcomes. The corresponding tree diagram is shown in Figure 5.

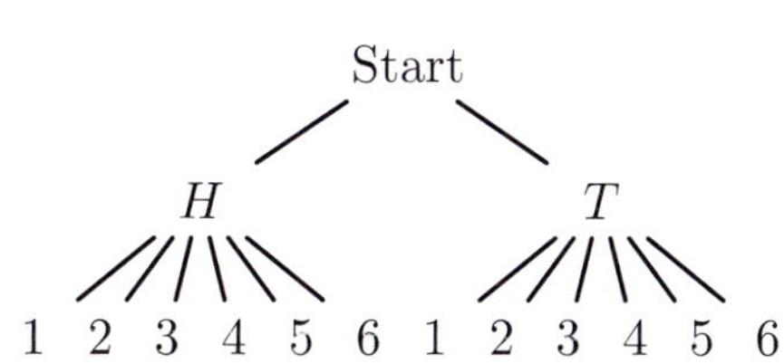

Figure 5 A tree diagram illustrating the possible outcomes from tossing a coin and rolling a die

The set of all possible outcomes is called the **sample space**. An **event** is a subset of the sample space (that is, a collection of possible outcomes).

In the scenario of a single coin toss and a roll of a die, the sample space S consists of the 12 possible outcomes

$$S = \{1H, 2H, 3H, 4H, 5H, 6H, 1T, 2T, 3T, 4T, 5T, 6T\},$$

where, for example, '$1H$' means the number 1 was rolled on the die and the coin landed showing heads. The event E that corresponds to 'The coin landed showing heads, and an even number was rolled on the die' is the subset of S given by

$$E = \{2H, 4H, 6H\}.$$

We now assume that each outcome in the sample space is equally likely to happen. This is a reasonable assumption to make: when we toss a coin, we expect that it is as likely to turn up heads as it is to turn up tails. Similarly, provided the die is not weighted, we expect each number to come up as often as any other number. Finally, we can combine the toss of a coin and the roll of a die and be sure that each of the 12 possible outcomes is equally likely to happen, because the outcome of the coin toss does not influence the outcome of rolling the die, and vice versa.

With the assumption that each outcome in the sample space is equally likely to happen, we can define the probability of an event.

The probability of an event

For a sample space S in which each outcome is equally likely, the **probability** that the event E happens is

$$P(E) = \frac{|E|}{|S|}.$$

Note that if the event E is equal to the whole sample space S, then the event E *must* happen, and this is exactly what $P(E) = 1$ means. On the other hand, if $E = \varnothing$, then the event *never* happens, and $P(E) = 0$. For any event E, we always have

$$0 \leq P(E) \leq 1.$$

In the example above of a single coin toss and a roll of a die, the probability that the coin comes up heads and an even number is rolled on the die is given by

$$\frac{|\{2H, 4H, 6H\}|}{|\{1H, 2H, 3H, 4H, 5H, 6H, 1T, 2T, 3T, 4T, 5T, 6T\}|} = \frac{3}{12} = \frac{1}{4}.$$

Example 10 *Finding probabilities when rolling dice*

Find the probability that the total will be less than 5 when the following numbers of dice are rolled.

(a) One die. (b) Two dice.

Solution

(a) The question is asking for the probability of rolling a 1, 2, 3 or 4 with a single die. First identify the sample space S, and the subset E of the sample space that corresponds to this event.

For one die, the sample space is

$$S = \{1, 2, 3, 4, 5, 6\}.$$

Check: is every outcome in the sample space equally likely? Yes.

The event that the roll of the die results in a number less than 5 is

$$E = \{1, 2, 3, 4\}.$$

Since $|S| = 6$ and $|E| = 4$, the probability is

$$P(\text{number rolled is less than } 5) = \tfrac{4}{6} = \tfrac{2}{3}.$$

(b) The question is asking for the probability that the total from a roll of two dice is 1, 2, 3 or 4. Here we can take the sample space to consist of pairs of numbers, where the first number is the number rolled on the first die, and the second number is the number rolled on the second die.

Let the sample space be

$$\begin{aligned} S = \{&(1,1),(1,2),\dots,(1,6),\\ &(2,1),(2,2),\dots,(2,6),\\ &\qquad\vdots\\ &(6,1),(6,2)\dots,(6,6)\}. \end{aligned}$$

Check: is every outcome in the sample space equally likely? Yes.

The outcomes in S are all equally likely to happen, because we are recording the roll of each die separately.

How many elements does S have? We could just count the elements above, or we can use the multiplication principle.

S has

$$|S| = 6 \times 6 = 36$$

elements, because there is a fixed number (6) of possible outcomes for the roll of each die, so we can apply the multiplication principle.

Now we need to work out the size of the event. Here, it seems easiest to list all the elements of the sample space for which the total of the numbers rolled is less than 5.

The event that the total of the numbers rolled on two dice is less than 5 is the set

$$E = \{(1,1), (1,2), (1,3), (2,1), (2,2), (3,1)\}.$$

Since $|E| = 6$, we have

$$P(\text{total rolled on two dice is less than 5}) = \tfrac{6}{36} = \tfrac{1}{6}.$$

Look again at the solution to part (b) of Example 10. We chose the sample space to consist of *pairs* of numbers, the first number corresponding to the roll of the first die, the second number to the roll of the second die.

Suppose that instead we chose the sample space

$$S = \{2, 3, \ldots, 12\},$$

which records the sum of the numbers on the two dice. In this case, the event would be $E = \{2, 3, 4\}$, from which we find $P(E) = \frac{3}{11}$, but this does not agree with the answer in the solution to the example.

The problem with this second approach is that the outcomes in the sample space are *not* equally likely. For example, there is only one way to achieve a total of 2 (namely by rolling a 1 on each die), whereas there are three ways to achieve a total of 4:

1 on the first die and 3 on the second die,

2 on the first die and 2 on the second die,

3 on the first die and 1 on the second die.

This demonstrates why you need to check whether the outcomes in your sample space are all equally likely. Now here's an activity for you to try.

Activity 17 *Finding probabilities when tossing a coin*

A coin is tossed five times. Calculate the probability of each of the following events.

(a) The coin lands showing heads every time.

(b) There is at least one head.

(c) There is exactly one head.

(d) There are at least two heads.

The UK National Lottery

A modern-day application of counting and probability is to calculate the chances of winning the UK National Lottery. You will see here how to calculate the chances of winning the big prize, as well as the chances of winning a smaller prize. Finally, you will be asked to work out the probability that you *don't* win the lottery!

Example 11 *Calculating the probability of winning the UK National Lottery*

Players of the main UK National Lottery purchase tickets on which they have to choose 6 different numbers from the numbers $1, 2, \ldots, 49$. In the draw, the winning 6 numbers are decided by randomly taking 6 different numbered balls from a drum containing a set of 49 balls numbered 1 to 49. Prizes are awarded for tickets that match 3 or more of the winning numbers, in whatever order.

(a) How many ways are there to pick numbers to play the UK National Lottery?

(b) What is the probability that a ticket matches all 6 winning numbers? Give your answer to three significant figures.

(c) What is the probability that a ticket matches exactly 3 of the winning numbers? Give your answer to three significant figures.

Solution

(a) There are 6 numbers to be chosen from 49 possible numbers, where the order does not matter and repetitions are not allowed.

The number of ways to pick the numbers for a ticket is equal to the number of combinations of 49 numbers taken 6 at a time. This is

$$^{49}C_6 = \frac{49 \times 48 \times 47 \times 46 \times 45 \times 44}{6 \times 5 \times 4 \times 3 \times 2 \times 1} = 13\,983\,816.$$

(b) We are asked to calculate the probability that a ticket matches the 6 winning numbers. For this, we can assume that the numbers on the ticket are 'fixed': that is, we have already bought a ticket, and are now waiting to hear the winning numbers announced.

The sample space S consists of all possible ways to draw 6 numbers from $\{1, 2, 3, \ldots, 49\}$, and since the Lottery can be assumed to be fair, each outcome is equally likely. The number of outcomes in S is given by the same calculation as in part (a).

The sample space S of all possible sets of 6 winning numbers contains $^{49}C_6 = 13\,983\,816$ outcomes, and all of these are equally likely.

Since all 6 winning numbers must be matched with the 6 on the player's ticket, the event E consists of exactly one of these outcomes.

The probability of matching all 6 winning numbers with a single ticket is therefore

$$\frac{|E|}{|S|} = \frac{1}{13\,983\,816} = 0.000\,000\,071\,5 \text{ (to 3 s.f.)}.$$

(c) The sample space is the same as in part (b). Note that we still treat the 6 numbers that are on our ticket as 'fixed', so we are looking at the possible ways that the three winning numbers can be drawn.

As before, take the sample space S to be the 13 983 816 different sets of 6 winning numbers.

The event E consists of all the different sets of 6 winning numbers for which exactly three match any of the 6 numbers that the player chose.

Counting the size of the event E looks rather complicated! Let's try rephrasing it by describing what a single outcome in E must consist of.

Put another way, each outcome in E will consist of any three of the 6 numbers on the player's ticket, and any three of the 43 numbers that the player didn't select.

The 6 numbers on the player's ticket are fixed, and so are the 43 that the player did not select. So elements of E are formed by choosing any 3 numbers from 6, followed by any 3 numbers from 43: this needs the multiplication principle.

There are ${}^6C_3 = 20$ ways to select the three numbers from the player's selection, and ${}^{43}C_3 = 12\,341$ ways to select the three numbers from those that the player did not pick. Therefore $|E| = {}^6C_3 \times {}^{43}C_3 = 246\,820$, by the multiplication principle.

Thus the probability of matching exactly three numbers is

$$\frac{|E|}{|S|} = \frac{246\,820}{13\,983\,816} = 0.0177 \text{ (to 3 s.f.)}.$$

The probability in part (c) above is approximately 1 in 57. So this means that, if you buy a lottery ticket every Saturday, you can expect to match 3 numbers roughly once every 57 weeks. Meanwhile, the probability of winning the jackpot is 1 in 13 983 816, which means you can expect to win the jackpot approximately once every 268 919 years!

Activity 18 *Calculating the probability of not winning the UK National Lottery!*

Calculate the probability that a single ticket on the UK National Lottery does *not* win a prize (that is, the ticket matches at most 2 of the winning numbers). Give your answer to three significant figures.

3 First-order recurrence systems

Often a particular counting problem is just one of a sequence of counting problems, in which there is one problem for each value of a variable n.

For instance, the problem

'How many permutations are there of the numbers 1, 2, 3, 4?'

is just one problem in the sequence of counting problems given by the question

'How many permutations are there of the numbers $1, 2, 3, \dots, n$?',

where n is a positive integer.

The answers to a sequence of counting problems form a sequence of numbers. For example, let a_n denote the number of permutations of all n of the numbers $1, 2, 3, \dots, n$. From the previous section, you know that $a_n = n!$. Thus the answers to the sequence of counting problems above form the sequence of numbers (a_n) where $a_n = n!$, which begins

$$1, 2, 6, 24, 120, 720, 5040, \dots .$$

In this section and the next, you'll learn some methods for answering questions that involve sequences of counting problems. Specifically, you'll learn how to construct and use first- and second-order recurrence systems to answer such questions. In this section, we'll focus on sequences of problems that have *first-order recurrence systems.*

Recall from Unit 10 of MST124 that a **first-order recurrence relation** for a sequence is an equation that expresses each term a_n of the sequence in terms of the previous term a_{n-1}. To specify a sequence using a **first-order recurrence system**, three pieces of information are needed:

- the value of the first term of the sequence
- a first-order recurrence relation for the sequence
- the range of values for the index variable in the recurrence relation.

(Recall that the **index variable** for a sequence (a_n) is the variable n in the notation a_n.)

A sequence that is specified by a recurrence system is called a **recurrence sequence**. For example, the sequence (a_n) above, whose nth term is $a_n = n!$, is a recurrence sequence that can be specified by the following first-order recurrence system:

$$a_1 = 1, \quad a_n = na_{n-1} \quad (n = 2, 3, 4, \dots).$$

In MST124 Unit 10, you were also introduced to the idea of a **closed form** for a sequence, which is a formula that defines the general term a_n as an expression involving the index variable n. To specify a sequence using a closed form, two pieces of information are needed: the closed form, and the range of values for the index variable in the closed form. If we can find a closed form for a recurrence sequence, then we say that we have **solved** the recurrence system.

For example, the recurrence sequence (a_n) above can be specified using the following closed form:

$$a_n = n! \quad (n = 1, 2, 3, \dots).$$

When you are faced with a sequence of counting problems, there are two steps to be carried out:

1. Use the information in the specification of the counting problems to find a recurrence system for the sequence formed by the answers to the counting problems.
2. If possible, solve the recurrence system to find a closed form.

You'll look at some techniques for carrying out the first of these two steps in Subsection 3.3. Before then, however, let's look at the second step. There is no general method that can be used to solve every first-order recurrence system, but we'll concentrate on one particular family of recurrence systems that can always be solved. This family can be thought of as a generalisation of both arithmetic and geometric sequences. As you'll see, the recurrence systems in this family occur in situations other than counting problems.

3.1 Combining arithmetic and geometric sequences

Recall from MST124 Unit 10 that an **arithmetic sequence** (x_n) is a sequence of numbers in which each successive term is formed by adding a constant d to the preceding term. In other words, the sequence satisfies a recurrence system of the form

$$x_1 = a, \quad x_n = x_{n-1} + d \quad (n = 2, 3, 4, \dots),$$

where a is the first term of the sequence. A closed form for the sequence specified by this recurrence system is

$$x_n = a + (n-1)d \quad (n = 1, 2, 3, \dots).$$

Similarly, a **geometric sequence** is a sequence of numbers in which each successive term is formed by multiplying the preceding term by a constant r. That is, the sequence satisfies a recurrence system of the form

$$x_1 = a, \quad x_n = rx_{n-1} \quad (n = 2, 3, 4, \dots),$$

where a is the first term of the sequence. A closed form for the sequence specified by this recurrence system is

$$x_n = ar^{n-1} \quad (n = 1, 2, 3, \dots).$$

To see how to combine the ideas behind arithmetic and geometric sequences, we'll look at two particular sequences as examples. First, consider the sequence that begins

6000, 6400, 6860, 7389, 7997, ...

This sequence represents the size of the deer population in successive years in a colony for which it is assumed that the annual increase in population from natural causes (births minus deaths) is 15%, but this is partially offset by a policy of culling 500 deer at the end of each year. The figure of 15% is based on historical observations, whereas the figure of 500 has been determined as a way of controlling the population. We'll call this sequence (P_n), so that $P_1 = 6000$, $P_2 = 6400$, $P_3 = 6860$, and so on.

To get from any term in this sequence to the next, we first *multiply* by a particular number, namely 1.15, and then *add* another number, namely -500:

$$1.15 \times 6000 - 500 = 6400,$$

$$1.15 \times 6400 - 500 = 6860,$$

$$1.15 \times 6860 - 500 = 7389,$$

and so on. The numbers 1.15 and -500 occur here because each year the natural increase is 0.15 (that is, 15%) of the size of the population at the start of the year, and there is a reduction of 500 at the end of the year due to the cull. (The terms of the sequence illustrated above have been rounded to the nearest integer where necessary, because the population of deer must be of integer size.)

The deer population sequence can therefore be described by the recurrence system

$$P_1 = 6000, \quad P_n = 1.15P_{n-1} - 500 \quad (n = 2, 3, 4, \ldots).$$

For our second example, consider the sequence

$$100\,000,\ 96\,975.74,\ 93\,800.27,\ 90\,466.02,\ \ldots,\ 7642.11,\ -0.04.$$

This represents the amount (in £) owing to a bank on 1 January of each year over the 20-year period of a mortgage, with a fixed interest rate of 5% per annum and total annual payments (interest plus partial repayment) of £8024.26. For simplicity, we've assumed that the borrower pays the amount due each year in one sum at the end of the year. We'll call this sequence (M_n), so that $M_1 = 100\,000$, $M_2 = 96\,975.74$, $M_3 = 93\,800.27$, and so on, as far as $M_{20} = 7642.11$ and $M_{21} = -0.04$.

The value $M_{21} = -0.04$ shows that, unless some adjustment is made, the borrower will have overpaid the bank by 4p at the end of the 20-year period! Ideally, we should have $M_{21} = 0$. The reason for this 'untidiness' will be discussed later. The terms of the sequence illustrated above have been rounded to the nearest penny, where necessary.

Once again, to get from any term in this sequence to the next, we first *multiply* by a particular number, namely 1.05, and then *add* another number, namely -8024.26:

$$1.05 \times 100\,000 - 8024.26 = 96\,975.74,$$

$$1.05 \times 96\,975.74 - 8024.26 = 93\,800.27,$$

$$1.05 \times 93\,800.27 - 8024.26 = 90\,466.02,$$

and so on. The number 1.05 appears here because the interest to be paid each year is 0.05 times the amount owing (that is, 5% of the amount owing) at the beginning of the year. The apparently arbitrary number 8024.26 has been carefully calculated by the bank so that at the end of the 20th year (which is also the beginning of the 21st year) the amount is reduced to approximately 0. Thus this sequence can be defined by the same kind of recurrence system as for the deer population: to get from one term in the sequence to the next, we first *multiply* by 1.05 and then *add* −8024.26. The corresponding recurrence system is

$$M_1 = 100\,000, \quad M_n = 1.05M_{n-1} - 8024.26 \quad (n = 2, 3, 4, \ldots, 21).$$

The final value in the range of the index variable n is 21 because the final term in the mortgage sequence is M_{21}, the amount (almost zero) owing at the beginning of the 21st year.

The deer population and mortgage sequences are both examples of sequences that have a recurrence system of the form

$$x_1 = a, \quad x_n = rx_{n-1} + d \quad (n = 2, 3, 4, \ldots), \tag{5}$$

where a is the first term, and r and d are constants, with $r \neq 0$.
A recurrence relation of the form in this recurrence system is a *linear first-order constant-coefficient recurrence relation.* This is rather a lot of words, but here's an explanation of what each word means.

Linear This means that the recurrence relation for x_n involves no powers of x_{n-1} other than x_{n-1} itself.

First-order This means that the recurrence relation for x_n involves only the immediately preceding term x_{n-1} in the sequence, and no others.

Note that a **second-order** recurrence relation involves the previous *two* terms x_{n-1} and x_{n-2}, and no others. Higher order recurrence relations are defined similarly. You'll learn about second-order recurrence relations in Section 4.

Constant-coefficient This means that the coefficient r of x_{n-1} is a constant, rather than a function of the index variable n.

For brevity, we'll refer to a recurrence relation of the form above, that is,

$$x_n = rx_{n-1} + d,$$

where r and d are constants with $r \neq 0$, simply as a **first-order recurrence relation**. Similarly, we'll refer to a sequence that has a recurrence relation of this form as a **first-order recurrence sequence**, and a recurrence system that includes a recurrence relation of this form as a **first-order recurrence system**.

You may be interested to know that a recurrence relation of the form above would still be a linear first-order constant-coefficient recurrence relation if it included a function of n in place of the constant term d. However, we do not consider recurrence relations of this type in this unit.

The values of a, r and d in recurrence system (5) determine a particular first-order recurrence sequence; we call a, r and d the **parameters** of the first-order recurrence sequence. For example, the deer population sequence has $a = 6000$, $r = 1.15$ and $d = -500$, while the mortgage sequence has $a = 100\,000$, $r = 1.05$ and $d = -8024.26$.

A first-order recurrence sequence (x_n) may be finite, as for the mortgage sequence, or infinite, as for the deer population sequence (if the circumstances determining the size of this population are assumed to continue forever). The first term is sometimes denoted by x_0 rather than x_1, in which case the sequence is given by

$$x_0 = a, \quad x_n = rx_{n-1} + d \quad (n = 1, 2, 3, \ldots).$$

Notice that

- arithmetic sequences (which have recurrence relations of the form $x_n = x_{n-1} + d$) are special cases of first-order recurrence sequences in which $r = 1$;
- geometric sequences (which have recurrence relations of the form $x_n = rx_{n-1}$) are special cases of first-order recurrence sequences in which $d = 0$.

So first-order recurrence sequences are indeed a generalisation of both arithmetic and geometric sequences.

Activity 19 *Recognising first-order recurrence systems*

Which of the following recurrence systems are first-order recurrence systems (that is, linear first-order constant-coefficient recurrence systems)? For each one that is, write down the values of the parameters a, r and d.

(a) $u_1 = 1, \quad u_n = 2u_{n-1} + 1 \quad (n = 2, 3, 4 \ldots)$

(b) $v_1 = 1, \quad v_n = -v_{n-1} - 1 \quad (n = 2, 3, 4 \ldots)$

(c) $w_0 = 2, \quad w_n = w_{n-1} - 1.5 \quad (n = 1, 2, 3 \ldots)$

(d) $x_0 = -1, \quad x_n = x_{n-1}^2 + 1 \quad (n = 1, 2, 3 \ldots)$

3.2 Solving first-order recurrence systems

In this subsection, you'll see how to solve first-order recurrence systems. In other words, given the parameters a, r and d in a first-order recurrence system, you'll see how to find a closed form for the sequence that it specifies. You can use the following fact.

Closed form for a first-order recurrence sequence

Suppose that the sequence (x_n) is given by the recurrence system

$$x_1 = a, \quad x_n = rx_{n-1} + d \quad (n = 2, 3, 4, \ldots),$$

where $r \neq 1$. Then a closed form for (x_n) is given by the formula

$$x_n = Cr^{n-1} + D \quad (n = 1, 2, 3, \ldots),$$

where C and D are constants.

For example, a closed form for the sequence (x_n) given by the recurrence system

$$x_1 = 4, \quad x_n = -2x_{n-1} + 3 \quad (n = 2, 3, 4, \dots),$$

is

$$x_n = 3 \times (-2)^{n-1} + 1 \quad (n = 1, 2, 3, \dots),$$

which is the formula in the box above with $C = 3$ and $D = 1$. You might like to check this closed form for the first few terms.

Note that, although the box above excludes the case $r = 1$, a first-order recurrence sequence where the parameter r is equal to 1 is an arithmetic sequence, so you already know to find a closed form for it.

The box tells you that every sequence with a recurrence relation $x_n = rx_{n-1} + d$, where $r \neq 1$, has a closed form given by the formula $x_n = Cr^{n-1} + D$, where C and D are constants. In other words, the **general solution** of the first-order recurrence relation $x_n = rx_{n-1} + d$, where $r \neq 1$, is $x_n = Cr^{n-1} + D$, where C and D are constants.

You'll see a proof of this fact shortly. First, however, let's look at how to find the constants C and D in a particular instance.

Example 12 *Finding a closed form for a first-order recurrence sequence*

Find a closed form for the sequence (x_n) given by the recurrence system

$$x_1 = 5, \quad x_n = 2x_{n-1} + 3 \quad (n = 2, 3, 4, \dots).$$

Solution

Find the first two terms.

The first two terms of the sequence are

$$x_1 = 5 \quad \text{and} \quad x_2 = 2 \times 5 + 3 = 13.$$

Use the fact in the box above. Here, $r = 2$.

A closed form for the sequence is

$$x_n = C \times 2^{n-1} + D,$$

where C and D are constants.

To find the constants C and D, substitute the first two terms of the sequence into the formula above.

The first term of the sequence is $x_1 = 5$, so substituting this and $n = 1$ into the formula gives

$$5 = C \times 2^0 + D;$$

that is,

$$C + D = 5. \tag{6}$$

The second term of the sequence is $x_2 = 13$, so substituting this and $n = 2$ into the formula gives

$$13 = C \times 2^1 + D,$$

that is,

$$2C + D = 13. \tag{7}$$

Solve the simultaneous linear equations (6) and (7).

Subtracting equation (6) from equation (7) gives $C = 8$.

Substituting into equation (6) gives

$$8 + D = 5,$$
$$D = -3.$$

So a closed form is

$$x_n = 8 \times 2^{n-1} - 3 \quad (n = 1, 2, 3, \dots).$$

Since $8 = 2^3$, this can be written as

$$x_n = 2^{n+2} - 3 \quad (n = 1, 2, 3, \dots).$$

Check the answer, by comparing the first two values given by the closed form with those given by the recurrence system.

To check this answer, the closed form gives $x_1 = 2^{1+2} - 3 = 8 - 3 = 5$ and $x_2 = 2^{2+2} - 3 = 16 - 3 = 13$, as expected.

To prove the formula for a closed form of a first-order recurrence sequence given in the box before Example 12, we make use of the formula for the sum of a finite geometric series, which was covered in MST124 Unit 10. Here's a reminder of the formula.

Sum of a finite geometric series

The geometric series with first term a, common ratio $r \neq 1$ and n terms has the sum

$$\frac{a(1 - r^n)}{1 - r}.$$

To begin the proof, suppose that the first-order recurrence sequence (x_n) is given by the recurrence system

$$x_1 = a, \quad x_n = rx_{n-1} + d \quad (n = 2, 3, 4, \dots),$$

with $r \neq 1$. Then

$$\begin{aligned}
x_1 &= a, \\
x_2 &= rx_1 + d = ra + d, \\
x_3 &= rx_2 + d = r(ra + d) + d = r^2a + rd + d, \\
x_4 &= rx_3 + d = r(r^2a + rd + d) + d = r^3a + r^2d + rd + d, \\
x_5 &= rx_4 + d = r(r^3a + r^2d + rd + d) + d = r^4a + r^3d + r^2d + rd + d,
\end{aligned}$$

and so on. You can see that, in general,

$$x_n = r^{n-1}a + r^{n-2}d + r^{n-3}d + \dots + rd + d.$$

Taking out the common factor d from the terms after the first term gives

$$x_n = r^{n-1}a + d(r^{n-2} + r^{n-3} + \dots + r + 1).$$

Rearranging the expression in the brackets in ascending powers of r, you can see that it is a geometric series with first term 1, common ratio r and $n - 1$ terms. Thus we can use the formula from the box above for the sum of a finite geometric series, which gives

$$\begin{aligned}
x_n &= r^{n-1}a + d\left(\frac{1 - r^{n-1}}{1 - r}\right) \\
&= r^{n-1}a + \frac{d}{1 - r} - \frac{dr^{n-1}}{1 - r} \\
&= \left(a - \frac{d}{1 - r}\right) r^{n-1} + \frac{d}{1 - r}. \qquad (8)
\end{aligned}$$

This expression is of the form $Cr^{n-1} + D$, where

$$C = a - \frac{d}{1 - r} \quad \text{and} \quad D = \frac{d}{1 - r}.$$

This proves that a closed form for (x_n) is

$$x_n = Cr^{n-1} + D \quad (n = 1, 2, 3, \dots)$$

where C and D are constants, as claimed earlier.

Notice that the proof actually provides us with a formula, namely expression (8), for a closed form for a first-order recurrence sequence, in terms of its parameters a, r and d. You can use this formula if you wish, but it's usually simpler to remember the expression $x_n = Cr^{n-1} + D$, and use the first two terms of the sequence to work out the values of C and D, as was done in Example 12.

Another way to solve recurrence systems is to use the computer algebra system. You will learn how to do that later, in Activity 31. For the time being, here are some problems for you to try by hand.

Activity 20 *Finding closed forms for first-order recurrence sequences*

(a) Find a closed form for the infinite first-order recurrence sequence (x_n) that begins

$$3,\ 5,\ 9,\ 17,\ \ldots,$$

and which has the recurrence system

$$x_1 = 3, \quad x_n = 2x_{n-1} - 1 \quad (n = 2, 3, 4, \ldots).$$

Check that your answer gives the correct value for the fourth term, and also calculate the 10th term of the sequence.

(b) Repeat part (a) for the infinite first-order recurrence sequence (y_n) that begins

$$12,\ -3,\ 2,\ \tfrac{1}{3},\ \ldots,$$

and which has the recurrence system

$$y_1 = 12, \quad y_n = -\tfrac{1}{3}y_{n-1} + 1 \quad (n = 2, 3, 4, \ldots).$$

Give y_{10} to three decimal places.

(c) Repeat part (a) for the infinite first-order recurrence sequence (z_n) that begins

$$0,\ 2,\ 0,\ 2,\ \ldots,$$

and which has the recurrence system

$$z_1 = 0, \quad z_n = -z_{n-1} + 2 \quad (n = 2, 3, 4, \ldots).$$

Activity 21 *Estimating the size of the deer population*

The size of the deer population described in Subsection 3.1 satisfies the recurrence system

$$P_1 = 6000, \quad P_n = 1.15P_{n-1} - 500 \quad (n = 2, 3, 4, \ldots),$$

where P_n is the population size at the start of year n. By first finding a corresponding closed form, estimate the size of this population after 10 years (that is, when $n = 11$), giving your answer to the nearest 10 deer.

Mortgage repayments

To conclude this subsection we return to mortgage sequences, one example of which was introduced in Subsection 3.1. We'll consider how a bank can calculate the appropriate annual repayment amounts for a borrower.

Suppose that the bank lends at a fixed annual interest rate p, that is, $100 \times p$ per cent. For example, if the interest rate is 5% per annum, then $p = 0.05$. Suppose also that the period over which the mortgage is to be repaid is T years. If £L is lent initially and the annual repayments are to be £R, then the sequence (M_n) of amounts in pounds owed to the bank at the beginning of year n is given by the recurrence system

$$M_1 = L, \quad M_n = (1+p)M_{n-1} - R \quad (n = 2, 3, 4, \ldots, T+1).$$

The parameters of this first-order recurrence sequence are therefore $a = L$, $r = 1 + p$ and $d = -R$.

The object of the exercise is that the debt should be repaid exactly after T years, which will be achieved provided that $M_{T+1} = 0$.

To find a formula for the required annual repayment R (in £) in terms of the other variables, let's start by finding a closed form for the sequence (M_n). We could do this by using the method of Example 12, but here it is easier to use formula (8) on page 53. By this formula, a closed form for the sequence (M_n) is

$$M_n = \left(a - \frac{d}{1-r}\right) r^{n-1} + \frac{d}{1-r},$$

where the parameters a, r and d are given by the expressions found above; that is, $a = L$, $r = 1 + p$ and $d = -R$. Substituting these expressions into the closed form gives

$$M_n = \left(L - \frac{-R}{1-(1+p)}\right)(1+p)^{n-1} + \frac{-R}{1-(1+p)}.$$

Simplifying gives the following closed form for the sequence (M_n):

$$M_n = \left(L - \frac{R}{p}\right)(1+p)^{n-1} + \frac{R}{p} \quad (n = 1, 2, 3, \ldots, T+1).$$

To ensure that the mortgage is paid off after T years, we need $M_{T+1} = 0$. That is,

$$\left(L - \frac{R}{p}\right)(1+p)^{T} + \frac{R}{p} = 0. \tag{9}$$

The initial loan L (in £), interest rate p and number of years T are all known, so this is an equation that can be solved to find the annual repayment amount R (in £). Expanding the brackets in equation (9) gives

$$L(1+p)^T - \frac{R}{p}(1+p)^T + \frac{R}{p} = 0,$$

and so

$$\frac{R}{p}\left((1+p)^T - 1\right) = L(1+p)^T,$$

which gives the following formula for R:

$$R = \frac{Lp(1+p)^T}{(1+p)^T - 1}.$$

We have shown the following.

If a loan of £L is made at a fixed annual interest rate of p (that is, $100p$ per cent), to be repaid fully over T years by equal annual repayments of £R at the end of each year, then the value of R is given by

$$R = \frac{Lp(1+p)^T}{(1+p)^T - 1}.$$

Activity 22 *Calculating the annual mortgage repayment amount*

(a) Verify that for the mortgage described in Subsection 3.1, with initial loan £100 000, fixed annual interest rate 5% and loan period 20 years, the annual repayment amount should be £8024.26.

(b) Find the total interest that the borrower pays over the 20 year loan period.

'He couldn't keep up the mortgage repayments'

You should have found in Activity 22 that, in order to pay off the debt after 20 years, annual repayments of £8024.258 719 . . . are required. However, for practical purposes, this has to be rounded to the nearest penny, to give £8024.26. The small resulting difference in the parameter $d = -R$ of the recurrence system is what causes the overpayment of 4p after 20 years that was pointed out earlier.

In practice, the annual repayment amount for a mortgage is usually divided into 12 equal monthly repayments. Furthermore, the calculation above is for a mortgage in which the interest rate remains fixed throughout. For a variable-rate mortgage, the bank will carry out a fresh calculation of this type on each occasion that the interest rate p is altered, where the parameter L in the formula for R becomes the remaining debt at the time of the change (in £), and the repayment period becomes the time remaining until the end of the original loan period.

3.3 Finding first-order recurrence systems for counting problems

So far in this section, you've learned how to find a closed form for a first-order linear recurrence sequence, given its recurrence system. It's now time to learn some techniques for *finding* recurrence systems to solve counting problems. We'll begin by looking at a celebrated counting problem.

The Towers of Hanoi

The *Towers of Hanoi* is a famous puzzle that involves three vertical pegs and n circular discs of different sizes. To begin with, all of the discs are threaded onto the first peg, arranged in order of size with the largest at the bottom and the smallest at the top. The aim of the puzzle is to move all the discs to the third peg, so that they are arranged in the same order. Discs can be moved only one at a time, from one peg to another peg, and larger discs can never be placed on top of smaller discs.

What is the minimum number of moves required to solve the puzzle? When $n = 1$, a single move suffices. The case $n = 2$ requires three moves, as illustrated in Figure 6.

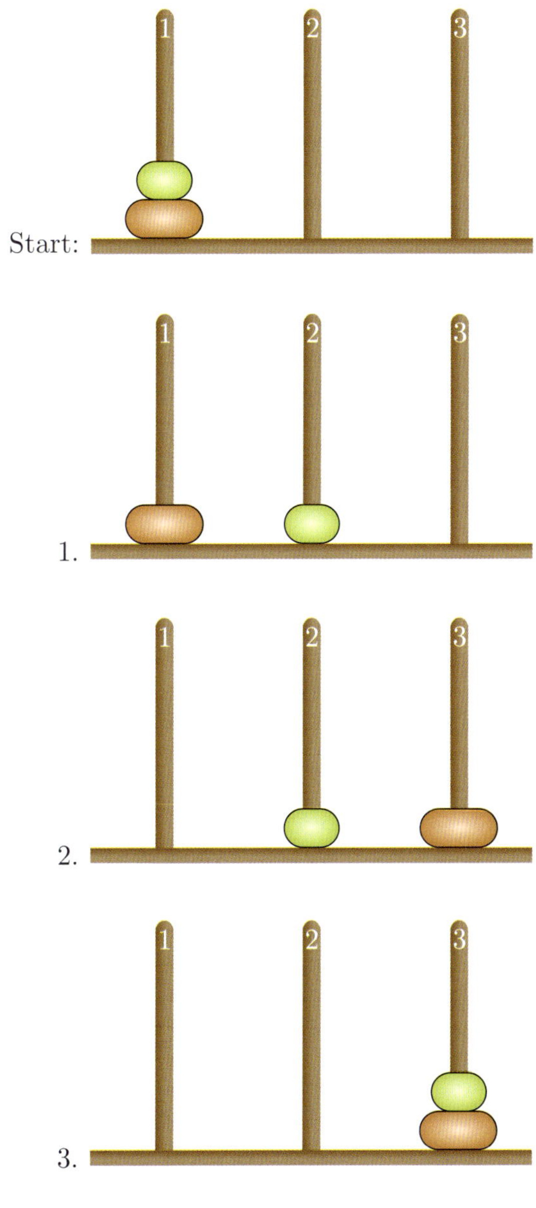

Figure 6 Solving the Towers of Hanoi puzzle with 2 discs

Activity 23 *Investigating the Towers of Hanoi puzzle*

Use the *Towers of Hanoi* applet to investigate the Towers of Hanoi puzzle. What is the minimum number of moves that you need to solve the puzzle for the case $n = 3$?

Let h_n denote the minimum number of moves required to solve the puzzle with n discs. You've already seen that, for $n = 1$, 2 and 3, the minimum numbers of moves are $h_1 = 1$, $h_2 = 3$ and $h_3 = 7$. Notice that

$$h_1 = 1 = 2^1 - 1,$$
$$h_2 = 3 = 2^2 - 1,$$
$$h_3 = 7 = 2^3 - 1,$$

so a reasonable conjecture to make is

$$h_n = 2^n - 1 \quad (n = 1, 2, 3, \dots).$$

In order to prove that this formula does indeed give the minimum number of moves required, let's construct a recurrence system for the sequence (h_n).

The first thing to do is to describe a strategy for solving the puzzle for a general value of n. Label the discs in order of increasing size as discs $1, 2, \dots, n$. The key observation to make is the following: we need to move the largest disc n only once, from the first peg to the third peg.

At the point when the largest disc n is moved in this way, all of discs $1, 2, 3, \dots, n - 1$ must be on the middle peg. So there is a solution to the puzzle that can be broken down into the following three steps, illustrated in Figure 7 for the case $n = 5$.

1. Make a sequence of moves that transfer the $n - 1$ smallest discs from peg 1 to peg 2 (Figure 7(a)–(b)).
2. Then make a single move that transfers the largest disc from peg 1 to peg 3 (Figure 7(b)–(c)).
3. Finally, make a sequence of moves that transfer the $n - 1$ smallest discs from peg 2 to peg 3 (Figure 7(c)–(d)).

(a) Initial position:

(b) Position after moving all but the largest disc to peg 2:

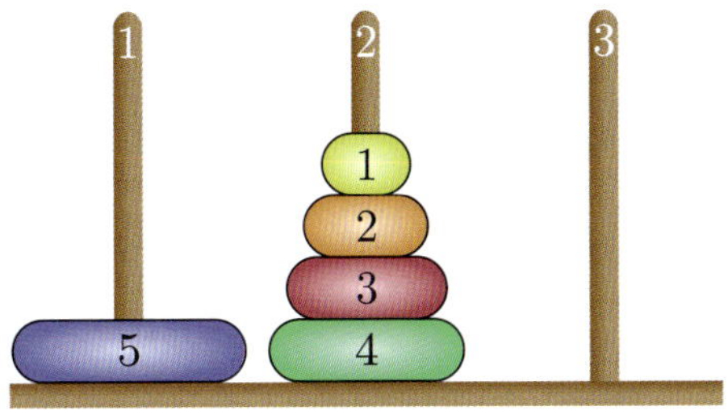

(c) Next step – move the largest disc to peg 3:

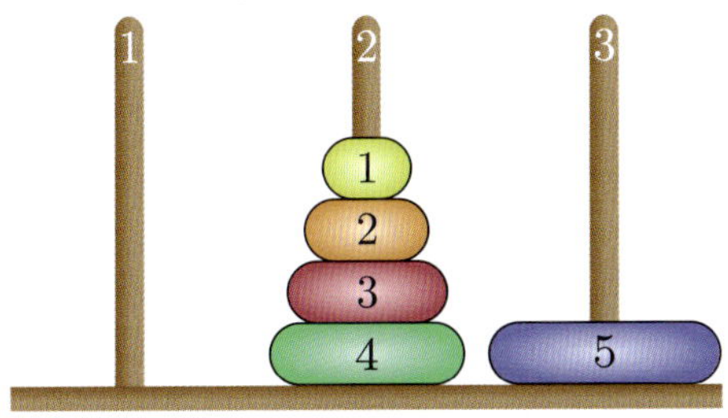

(d) Final position, after moving all the discs on peg 2 to peg 3:

Figure 7 A general approach to solving the Towers of Hanoi puzzle, illustrated for the case $n = 5$

Let's count the minimum number of moves that this solution takes.

First notice that, in any solution of the puzzle, the largest disc *must* move at least once, and each time the largest disc is transferred from one peg to another, the $n - 1$ smallest discs must all be stacked on the one remaining peg not involved in this move. In our solution, the largest disc moves exactly once, so this number is as small as possible. Consequently, the total number of moves in our solution will also be as small as possible if we ensure that the $n - 1$ smallest discs are transferred to and from the remaining peg using the minimum number of moves.

Now, transferring the $n-1$ smallest discs from peg 1 to peg 2 amounts to the same thing as solving the Towers of Hanoi puzzle for $n-1$ discs. To convince yourself of this, note that the original puzzle could equally well have been described in terms of moving discs from the first peg to the second peg: all that has changed is to swap the roles of the second and third pegs, so the number of moves is the same. Thus the minimum number of moves required for step 1 of our solution is h_{n-1}.

In exactly the same way, transferring the $n-1$ smallest discs from peg 2 to peg 3 also amounts to the same thing as solving the Towers of Hanoi puzzle for $n-1$ discs. Hence the minimum number of moves required for step 3 of our solution is also h_{n-1}.

Adding the single move required for step 2 of our solution gives the following recurrence relation:

$$h_n = h_{n-1} + 1 + h_{n-1};$$

that is,

$$h_n = 2h_{n-1} + 1.$$

Since $h_1 = 1$, we therefore have the following recurrence system for the minimum number of moves required to solve the Towers of Hanoi puzzle with n discs:

$$h_1 = 1, \quad h_n = 2h_{n-1} + 1 \quad (n = 2, 3, 4, \ldots) \tag{10}$$

Activity 24 *Solving the Towers of Hanoi problem*

Use recurrence system (10) to find a closed form for h_n.

Édouard Lucas (1842–1891)

The legend of the Towers of Hanoi

The Towers of Hanoi puzzle was introduced in Europe in 1883 by the French mathematician Édouard Lucas. The following year, another Frenchman, Henri de Parville, gave an elaborate account of its origins (though it's possible that he invented this account!). He tells of a legend in which Indian priests have a room with three posts and a stack of 64 golden discs, which they are moving according to the rules of the puzzle, as laid out by the Hindu god Brahma. The legend says that the world will end when the final move of the puzzle is made.

However, even if the priests manage 1 move per second, it will take them approximately 585 billion years to make the

$$2^{64} - 1 = 18\,446\,744\,073\,709\,551\,615$$

moves that the puzzle requires!

More complicated recurrence systems

For the Towers of Hanoi puzzle, the recurrence system turned out to be of the standard form

$$x_1 = a, \quad x_n = rx_{n-1} + d \quad (n = 2, 3, 4, \dots),$$

so you were able to find a closed form using the method from Subsection 3.2.

There are, of course, many counting problems for which you end up finding recurrence systems that are not of this form. An example of a recurrence system that is not of this form is

$$x_1 = 2, \quad x_n = x_{n-1}^2 \quad (n = 2, 3, 4, \dots). \tag{11}$$

This is an example of a *non-linear* first-order recurrence system, because of the squared term in the recurrence relation. This sequence begins

$$2, 4, 16, 256, \dots,$$

from which you might be able to guess (correctly) that a closed form for the sequence is

$$x_n = 2^{(2^{n-1})} \quad (n = 1, 2, 3, \dots).$$

On the other hand, the non-linear first-order recurrence system

$$y_1 = 1, \quad y_n = y_{n-1}^2 + 1 \quad (n = 2, 3, 4, \dots),$$

is not so easily expressed in closed form, despite its similarity to recurrence system (11).

In fact, there is no known general method for finding a closed form for a recurrence system. For the rest of this section, therefore, you'll be learning how to *find* first-order recurrence systems for counting problems, but you won't need to find a closed form. This is still a useful thing to do, because a recurrence system still provides an answer to a counting problem, even if it is less convenient than a closed form.

Here is an example.

Example 13 *Finding a recurrence system to count the number of regions created using straight lines*

(a) Find a recurrence system for the number of regions into which the plane is divided by n infinite straight lines, where every two lines intersect but no three lines meet at a point.

(b) How many regions are there with 8 straight lines?

Solution

(a) Let a_n denote the number of regions created from n lines.

Get a feel for the problem by working out the first few values.

The first few values of a_n are found below:

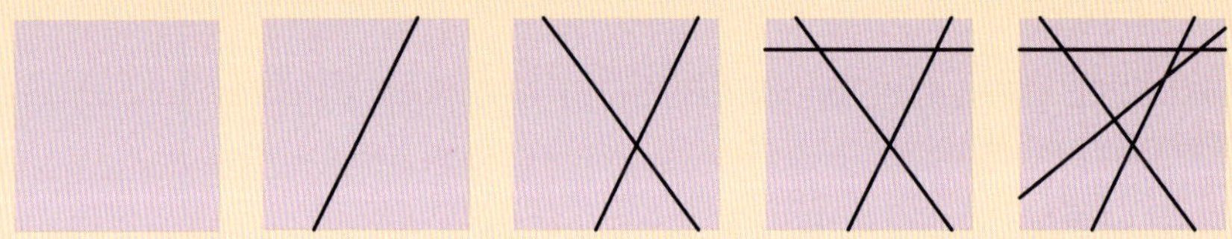

$a_0 = 1$ $a_1 = 2$ $a_2 = 4$ $a_3 = 7$ $a_4 = 11$

Try to spot a pattern in the sequence. An approach that can be helpful is to compute the difference between consecutive terms of the sequence, as follows:

n	0	1	2	3	4
a_n	1	2	4	7	11
$a_n - a_{n-1}$		1	2	3	4

So the first five values satisfy the recurrence relation $a_n = a_{n-1} + n$.

We will show that a_n satisfies the recurrence system

$$a_0 = 1, \quad a_n = a_{n-1} + n \quad (n = 1, 2, 3, \ldots).$$

This recurrence system says that when the plane contains $n - 1$ lines, n new regions are created when one extra line is added. The diagram below illustrates the case $n = 5$.

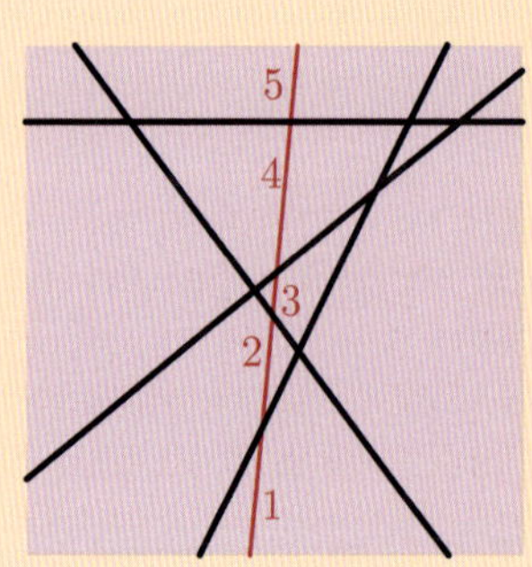

The red line has been added to intersect all 4 of the black lines, in such a way that it does not pass through the intersection point of any two black lines. The result is that the 4 black lines divide the red line into 5 line segments. Each of these 5 line segments cuts a different region into two pieces, so there are now 5 more regions than there were before the red line was added. This is still true when we replace '5' with 'n' and '4' with '$n-1$' throughout.

Consider an arrangement of $n-1$ lines that satisfies the conditions of the problem. By definition, the plane is divided into a_{n-1} regions. When a new line is added, it must intersect each of the existing $n-1$ lines, avoiding existing intersection points. These $n-1$ intersections divide the new line into n line segments, and so the new line passes through n regions of the original arrangement.

Since each region that the new line passes through is divided into two, the addition of this line creates n extra regions, so

$$a_n = a_{n-1} + n.$$

Since $a_0 = 1$, the recurrence system is

$$a_0 = 1, \quad a_n = a_{n-1} + n \quad (n = 1, 2, 3, \ldots).$$

(b) Starting from the initial condition $a_0 = 1$, use the recurrence relation repeatedly until a_8 is reached.

$$\begin{aligned}
a_1 &= 1 + 1 = 2\\
a_2 &= 2 + 2 = 4\\
a_3 &= 4 + 3 = 7\\
a_4 &= 7 + 4 = 11\\
a_5 &= 11 + 5 = 16\\
a_6 &= 16 + 6 = 22\\
a_7 &= 22 + 7 = 29\\
a_8 &= 29 + 8 = 37
\end{aligned}$$

So 8 lines divide the plane into 37 regions.

When you're trying to find an recurrence relation, although it's not essential to start by trying to spot a pattern and guess the recurrence relation, doing this can help you understand how to approach the problem, as in the example above. However, remember that you still need to show *why* the recurrence relation is what you claim it to be; your guess does not *prove* this!

The next activity is about the number of regions into which the plane is divided by n *circles*, rather than by n straight lines. The circles are drawn so that every two circles intersect in two places, but no three circles meet at a point. You should use a similar approach to that used in Example 13.

Let c_n denote the number of regions into which the plane is divided by n such circles. For example, $c_1 = 2$, because a single circle divides the plane into two regions – the inside of the circle and the outside. Figure 8 illustrates the fact that $c_2 = 4$.

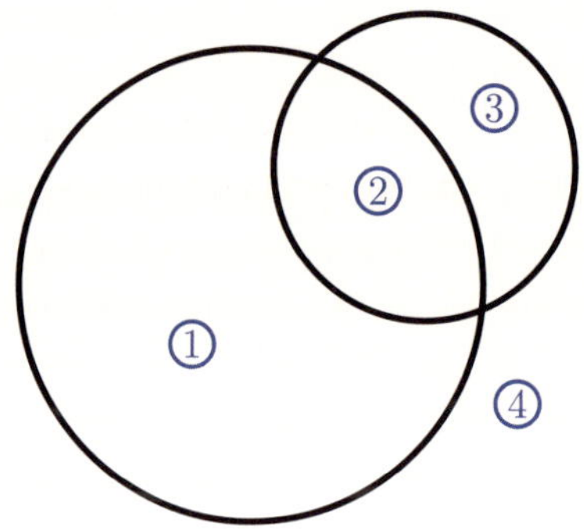

Figure 8 Two circles divide the plane into four regions

Some older textbooks on geometry say that objects are in **general position** if they intersect in pairs, but no three of them intersect at a point.

You may be wondering if it's possible to draw as many circles as you want to satisfy these conditions. Certainly as the number of circles increases you'll find it quite hard to draw, but in fact it is always possible. For the next activity you can assume that this is true.

Activity 25 *Counting the number of regions created using circles*

Let c_n denote the number of regions into which the plane is divided by n circles, drawn in such a way that every pair of circles intersect in two places but no three circles meet at a point.

(a) Find c_3, and make a conjecture for the nth term of the sequence, c_n.

(b) Now find c_4. Is your conjecture true for $n = 4$?

(c) Find a recurrence system for c_n.

(d) How many regions is the plane divided into when $n = 6$?

Before looking at another example of finding a recurrence system for a counting problem, you may find it useful to read through the following summary of how to proceed.

Strategy:
To find a first-order recurrence system for a sequence of counting problems

Suppose that the sequence (x_n) counts the number of objects with some property that depends on n. To find a first-order recurrence system for (x_n), proceed as follows.

1. Find the first two or three values of x_n by listing the objects. This will give you a feeling for the problem.
2. It may also help to try to find a way of visualising the problem using a diagram.
3. Try to express the number of objects counted by x_n in terms of the number of objects counted by x_{n-1}. That is, try to find a recurrence relation satisfied by the sequence (x_n).
   - Make sure that you give a clear, logical argument (a proof) that the recurrence relation is correct.
   - It may help to divide the problem into several cases and use the addition principle.
   - Sometimes it may help to count the objects *not* being counted by x_n, and use the subtraction principle.
4. As a check, determine whether the recurrence relation works for the first few values of n.
5. Specify the required recurrence system by giving the following:
   - the value of the first term in the sequence
   - the recurrence relation
   - the range of values for the index variable n.

Of course, sometimes it may be difficult or impossible to find a first-order recurrence system (or any recurrence system) for a particular sequence of counting problems.

Example 14 *Placing tigers in enclosures*

A zookeeper has n empty enclosures in a row, in which he wishes to keep two tigers. The tigers need to be kept apart, so they cannot be placed in the same enclosure, or in neighbouring enclosures.

Let t_n denote the number of acceptable ways of arranging the tigers in the n enclosures. Note that we don't distinguish between the two tigers, so we don't create a new arrangement simply by swapping the positions of the two tigers.

(a) Find t_1, t_2, t_3 and t_4.

(b) By dividing the permitted arrangements into two cases depending on whether or not the last enclosure in the row contains a tiger, show that the sequence (t_n) satisfies the recurrence system

$$t_1 = 0, \quad t_n = t_{n-1} + n - 2 \quad (n = 2, 3, 4, \dots).$$

(c) How many ways are there to place the tigers in a row of 8 enclosures?

Solution

(a) It often helps to find a way of illustrating a counting problem. In this case, we'll use a row of square boxes to illustrate the enclosures, and put the letter 'T' in a box to indicate there is a tiger in that enclosure. For example,

indicates a permitted arrangement of tigers in a collection of 6 enclosures, while

illustrates a forbidden arrangement, because the tigers are in neighbouring enclosures.

With one or two enclosures, it's impossible to keep two tigers since they couldn't be kept apart, so $t_1 = t_2 = 0$.

For three enclosures, there is exactly one way to keep the two tigers, as illustrated by the following diagram.

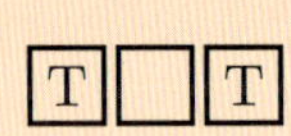

Therefore, $t_3 = 1$.

For four enclosures, there are three ways, illustrated below.

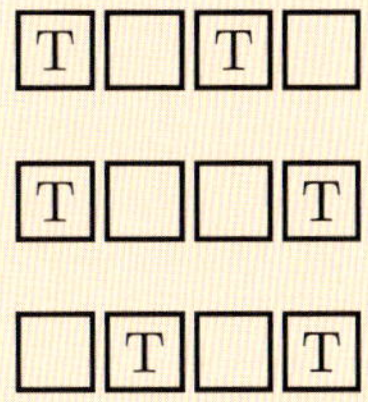

Therefore, $t_4 = 3$.

(b) The question suggests that we should try dividing the problem into two cases, depending on whether or not there is a tiger in the last of a row of n enclosures.

Let's start with the case that there is no tiger in the last enclosure. This means that both tigers must be arranged in the remaining $n - 1$ enclosures, in such a way that they are not in neighbouring enclosures. The trick now is to notice that the number of ways of arranging two tigers in these $n - 1$ enclosures is just t_{n-1}.

If there is no tiger in the last enclosure, we have the following situation.

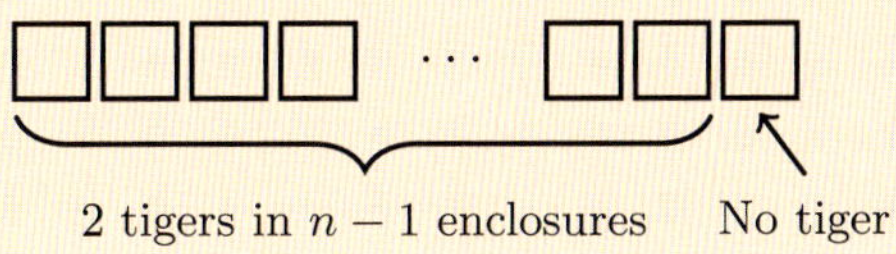

From this diagram, there are t_{n-1} possible arrangements of two tigers in n enclosures, when there is no tiger in the last enclosure.

For the case where there is a tiger in the last enclosure, we need to count the number of ways of placing the other tiger. This tiger can go anywhere, except for the last but one enclosure.

If there is a tiger in the last enclosure, we have the following situation.

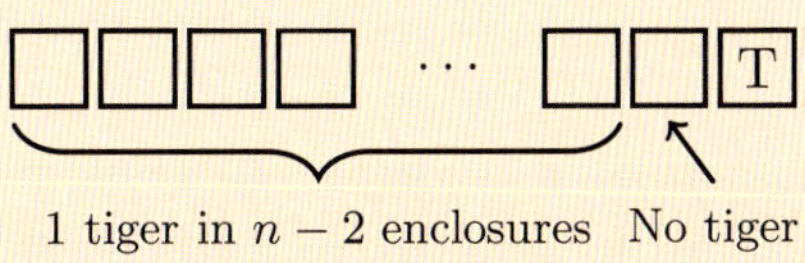

From this diagram, there are $n - 2$ possible enclosures that the other tiger can be placed in. Therefore, there are $n - 2$ possible arrangements of two tigers in n enclosures, when there is a tiger in the last enclosure.

Now we need to recombine these two cases. Notice that the two cases cover every possibility, because there must either be a tiger in the last enclosure or not. Thus the corresponding sets of ways of arranging the two tigers are disjoint, and we can use the addition principle.

Every arrangement of two tigers in n enclosures either has a tiger in the last enclosure or it doesn't, so the sets of possible arrangements in the two cases above are disjoint and cover every possible arrangement. Therefore we can apply the addition principle, and we conclude that t_n satisfies the recurrence relation

$$t_n = t_{n-1} + n - 2.$$

Finally, we need to specify the starting value for the recurrence relation, and the range of values for n. For the problem here it doesn't make sense to start with the value of t_0. This is because the only sensible value for t_0 is $t_0 = 0$, because there are no ways to place tigers in 0 enclosures, but the recurrence relation doesn't work if we substitute this value of t_0 (it gives $t_1 = -1$, which is incorrect). Hence we start the recurrence system with $t_1 = 0$, for which the recurrence relation does work.

The recurrence relation is valid for $n \geq 2$. By part (a) we know that $t_1 = 0$, so the recurrence system is

$$t_1 = 0, \quad t_n = t_{n-1} + n - 2 \quad (n = 2, 3, 4, \ldots).$$

(c) Use the recurrence system from part (b) to find t_8, by calculating $t_1, \ldots, t_7$ first.

$$\begin{aligned}
t_1 &= 0\\
t_2 &= 0 + (2 - 2) = 0\\
t_3 &= 0 + (3 - 2) = 1\\
t_4 &= 1 + (4 - 2) = 3\\
t_5 &= 3 + (5 - 2) = 6\\
t_6 &= 6 + (6 - 2) = 10\\
t_7 &= 10 + (7 - 2) = 15\\
t_8 &= 15 + (8 - 2) = 21.
\end{aligned}$$

Therefore there are 21 ways of arranging the two tigers in eight enclosures.

In the final activity of this section, you'll be guided step by step through the process of finding a recurrence system for another counting problem.

Activity 26 *Counting sequences of letters containing an odd number of As*

Let x_n denote the number of sequences of n letters from the set $\{A, B, C, D\}$ that contain an odd number of As, and let y_n be the number of sequences of n letters from the same set that contain either an even number of As, or no As at all.

(a) Find x_1, x_2, y_1 and y_2.

(b) Explain why, for $n \geq 1$,

$$y_n = 4^n - x_n.$$

(c) By considering whether the final letter of a sequence of n letters is A, B, C or D, show that

$$x_n = 3x_{n-1} + y_{n-1} \quad (n = 2, 3, 4, \dots).$$

(d) Hence, show that x_n satisfies the recurrence system

$$x_1 = 1, \quad x_n = 2x_{n-1} + 4^{n-1} \quad (n = 2, 3, 4, \dots).$$

(e) Use this recurrence system to find x_6, the number of 6-letter sequences containing an odd number of As.

4 Second-order recurrence systems

In the previous section, you learned about first-order recurrence sequences, that is, sequences whose nth term can be written in terms of the $(n-1)$th term. In this section, you'll investigate **second-order recurrence sequences**, that is, sequences whose nth term can be written in terms of the $(n-1)$th and the $(n-2)$th terms.

4.1 The Fibonacci sequence

Consider the following counting problem, posed by Leonardo of Pisa in 1202.

> **The rabbit problem**
>
> One pair of adult rabbits is kept in a field in isolation from any other rabbits except for their descendants. Suppose we make the following assumptions.
>
> - This pair of adult rabbits produces a new pair of rabbits in the first month, and in each subsequent month.
> - Each new pair becomes adult after one month and produces its first new pair in its second month, and a new pair in each subsequent month.
> - No rabbits die.
>
> How many pairs of rabbits are there after a year?

This is not a realistic problem about rabbit breeding, but the description does give it a memorable context!

Consider how the number of pairs of rabbits develops month by month. One new pair is born in the first month, so then there are two pairs. In month 2, the original adult pair produces another pair, so there are then 3 pairs. In month 3, the original adult pair produces yet another pair, and the pair born in month 1 reaches adulthood and so also produces a pair, making 5 pairs in all. This development is shown in Figure 9, where adult pairs are shown as solid circles and new pairs as empty circles.

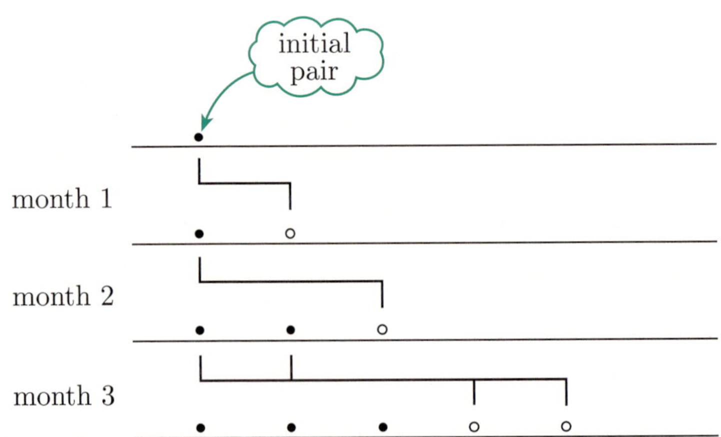

Figure 9 Number of pairs of rabbits at ends of months 1 to 3

In general, we see that at the end of each month:

- the number of adult pairs is equal to the total number of pairs at the end of the previous month,
- the number of new pairs is equal to the number of adult pairs at the end of the previous month.

Using these two observations, we obtain the results in Table 2.

Table 2 Rabbit pairs at the end of each month

Month	1	2	3	4	5	6	7	8	9	10	11	12
Adult pairs	1	2	3	5	8	13	21	34	55	89	144	233
New pairs	1	1	2	3	5	8	13	21	34	55	89	144
Total pairs	2	3	5	8	13	21	34	55	89	144	233	377

The entry at the bottom right of this table shows that the answer to Leonardo's question is 377.

Leonardo of Pisa (circa 1170–1250)

Leonardo of Pisa was one of the greatest mathematicians of the Middle Ages. He was educated in North Africa, where his father worked in commerce. He is more well known to us under the name Fibonacci, which is thought to be a contraction of *filius Bonacci*, meaning 'son of the Bonacci family.'

His book *Liber Abaci* ('Book of Calculation'), where the rabbit problem was first described, appeared in 1202. The book explains methods of arithmetic and algebra from the Arabic world, and its use of the Hindu–Arabic numerals $0, 1, 2, \ldots, 9$ to represent numbers in positional notation contributed to the dissemination of these numerals throughout Europe.

Leonardo of Pisa (circa 1170–1250)

The number patterns in Table 2 are striking. The final three rows of the table all contain essentially the same sequence of positive integers $1, 1, 2, 3, 5, 8, 13, \ldots$, each term of which (after the second) is the sum of the two previous terms:

$$2 = 1 + 1, \quad 3 = 2 + 1, \quad 5 = 3 + 2, \quad 8 = 5 + 3, \quad 13 = 8 + 5, \ldots .$$

This suggests that the rabbit problem satisfies a recurrence relation involving the previous two terms of the sequence, and the example below shows you how to prove that this is indeed the case.

'I'm only gonna say this one more time: our only chance is self-control'

Example 15 *Finding a recurrence system for the rabbit problem*

Show that the sequence (R_n) for the total number of pairs of rabbits at the end of month n satisfies the recurrence system

$$R_1 = 2, \quad R_2 = 3, \quad R_n = R_{n-1} + R_{n-2} \quad (n = 3, 4, 5, \ldots).$$

Solution

The recurrence system that we are trying to prove for R_n involves both R_{n-1} and R_{n-2}, so we need to explain where these come from. In each column of Table 2, the total number of pairs is equal to the sum of the number of adult pairs and the number of new pairs.

At the end of month n, the R_n pairs of rabbits can be divided into two types: adult pairs and new pairs (that is, those born during that month).

The number of adult pairs at the end of month n is equal to the total number of pairs (both adult pairs and new pairs) at the end of month $n - 1$. That is, there are R_{n-1} adult pairs at the end of month n.

The number of new pairs born in month n is equal to the number of *adult* pairs at the end of month $n - 1$. By the argument above, there are R_{n-2} adult pairs at the end of month $n - 1$, and so there are R_{n-2} new pairs at the end of month n.

When we add the number of adult pairs to the number of new pairs, we are using the addition principle.

Hence, by the addition principle, the total number of pairs at the end of month n is $R_n = R_{n-1} + R_{n-2}$.

The recurrence relation for R_n uses the previous two terms of the sequence, so the first *two* values of the sequence need to be given to specify the recurrence system.

The first two terms can be calculated directly (as shown in Table 2), and are $R_1 = 2$ and $R_2 = 3$. Thus the recurrence system for the rabbit problem is

$$R_1 = 2, \quad R_2 = 3, \quad R_n = R_{n-1} + R_{n-2} \quad (n = 3, 4, 5, \ldots).$$

A recurrence relation such as $R_n = R_{n-1} + R_{n-2}$, where each term depends on the previous two terms and no others, is called a **second-order recurrence relation**, and a corresponding recurrence system is called a **second-order recurrence system**. As illustrated in Example 15, a second-order recurrence system needs to include the values of *two* initial terms, that is, the first two terms of the sequence.
A sequence, such as (R_n), that satisfies a second-order recurrence system is called a **second-order recurrence sequence**.

Now consider the related sequence (F_n) counting the number of new pairs at the end of month n. From Table 2, this sequence begins

$$1, 1, 2, 3, 5, 8, 13, \ldots.$$

Notice that for $n \geq 1$, we have $F_{n+2} = R_n$, so the sequence (F_n) satisfies the same recurrence relation as (R_n), but it has different initial terms, namely $F_1 = 1$ and $F_2 = 1$. Consequently, it is given by the recurrence system

$$F_1 = 1, \quad F_2 = 1, \quad F_n = F_{n-1} + F_{n-2} \quad (n = 3, 4, 5, \ldots). \tag{12}$$

The sequence (F_n) is called the **Fibonacci sequence**. This name was first used by the French mathematician Édouard Lucas in 1877. The terms of the sequence are called **Fibonacci numbers**. Table 3 lists the first 14 Fibonacci numbers.

Table 3 Fibonacci numbers

n	1	2	3	4	5	6	7	8	9	10	11	12	13	14
F_n	1	1	2	3	5	8	13	21	34	55	89	144	233	377

You are now asked to calculate two more Fibonacci numbers.

Activity 27 *Calculating two more Fibonacci numbers*

Use the Fibonacci recurrence relation to calculate F_{15} and F_{16}.

4.2 Solving second-order recurrence systems

The Fibonacci recurrence relation $F_n = F_{n-1} + F_{n-2}$ is a particular example of a recurrence relation of the form

$$u_n = pu_{n-1} + qu_{n-2}, \tag{13}$$

where the coefficients p and q are constants, and $q \neq 0$. For the Fibonacci recurrence relation, $p = 1$ and $q = 1$.

The full name of such a recurrence relation is a **linear second-order constant-coefficient homogeneous recurrence relation**.
The meanings of the words *linear* and *constant-coefficient* are similar to their meanings for first-order recurrence relations, given on page 49, but you haven't yet met the term *homogeneous*. The meanings of all three words are as follows.

Linear This means that the recurrence relation involves no powers of u_{n-1} or u_{n-2} other than u_{n-1} and u_{n-2} themselves.

Constant-coefficient This means that the coefficients of u_{n-1} and u_{n-2} (that is, p and q) are constants, not functions of n.

Homogeneous This means that all the terms on the right-hand side of the recurrence relation involve u_{n-1} or u_{n-2}.

(Similarly, a *first-order* recurrence relation of the form $x_n = rx_{n-1} + d$ is *homogeneous* if all the terms on the right-hand side involve x_{n-1}. In other words, it is homogeneous if $d = 0$. So most of the first-order recurrence relations that you met in the previous section were not homogeneous.)

All the second-order recurrence relations that you'll see in this unit will be of form (13). So, for brevity, we'll refer to a recurrence relation of this form simply as a **second-order recurrence relation**. Similarly, we'll refer to a sequence that has a recurrence relation of this form as a **second-order recurrence sequence**, and a recurrence system that includes a recurrence relation of this form as a **second-order recurrence system**.

As mentioned earlier, to specify a second-order recurrence system we need to give the values of *two* initial terms. These are usually either the terms u_1 and u_2, as with the Fibonacci recurrence system (12), or the terms u_0 and u_1, as in the following recurrence system:

$$u_0 = a, \quad u_1 = b, \quad u_n = pu_{n-1} + qu_{n-2} \quad (n = 2, 3, 4, \dots). \tag{14}$$

The precise way in which a recurrence system is specified may depend on the problem from which it arises. Often, it doesn't make practical sense to have a 0th term of the sequence. However, as you'll see later when finding closed forms for second-order recurrence systems, sometimes the algebra is easier if an extra 0th term is included at the beginning of the sequence.

For the Fibonacci numbers we have $F_1 = 1$ and $F_2 = 1$, and we can find a 0th term F_0 by rearranging the recurrence relation as follows:

$$F_{n-2} = F_n - F_{n-1}.$$

This gives

$$F_0 = F_2 - F_1 = 1 - 1 = 0.$$

We can then specify the Fibonacci sequence using a recurrence system that starts at the 0th term:

$$F_0 = 0, \quad F_1 = 1, \quad F_n = F_{n-1} + F_{n-2} \quad (n = 2, 3, 4, \dots).$$

This section is about finding closed forms for some second-order recurrence systems. If we can find such a closed form, then we say that we have **solved** the recurrence system.

For the second-order recurrence systems you'll meet in this unit, it will always be possible to find a closed form. However, just as you saw in Section 3 for first-order recurrence systems, there is no systematic method for solving general second-order recurrence systems – remember that these may not necessarily be linear, or constant coefficient, or homogeneous.

In the next activity, you'll investigate closed forms for some second-order recurrence sequences by looking for patterns in the sequences.

Activity 28 *Looking for patterns in second-order recurrence sequences*

Consider the following recurrence relation:

$$u_n = 12u_{n-1} - 20u_{n-2} \quad (n = 2, 3, 4, \dots).$$

(a) For each of the following pairs of initial terms u_0 and u_1, find the terms u_2, u_3 and u_4 and enter them in the table.

	u_0	u_1	u_2	u_3	u_4
(i)	1	2			
(ii)	1	10			
(iii)	2	12			
(iv)	3	22			

(b) For sequences (i) and (ii), make a conjecture for a closed form for the nth term, u_n.

(c) Look at sequence (iii). What do you notice about the terms u_2, u_3 and u_4 in relation to the corresponding terms in sequences (i) and (ii)?

Make a conjecture for a closed form for the nth term of sequence (iii).

(d) Can you guess a formula for the nth term of sequence (iv)?

In the activity above, you made some conjectures about closed forms for the recurrence relation

$$u_n = 12u_{n-1} - 20u_{n-2} \quad (n = 2, 3, 4, \dots), \qquad (15)$$

for various values of u_0 and u_1.

Now let's see if we can confirm these conjectures by looking more closely at recurrence relation (15).

Suppose this recurrence relation is satisfied by a geometric sequence, say $u_n = r^n$ for some non-zero number r. Substituting $u_n = r^n$ into recurrence relation (15) yields

$$r^n = 12r^{n-1} - 20r^{n-2}.$$

Since $r \neq 0$, we can divide this whole equation through by r^{n-2} to get

$$r^2 = 12r - 20,$$

and by rearranging we obtain the quadratic equation

$$r^2 - 12r + 20 = 0.$$

This quadratic equation is called the *auxiliary equation* of recurrence relation (15). There is a formal definition of the auxiliary equation in the following box.

The auxiliary equation of a second-order recurrence relation

The **auxiliary equation** of the second-order recurrence relation

$$u_n = pu_{n-1} + qu_{n-2} \quad (n = 2, 3, 4, \dots)$$

is the quadratic equation

$$r^2 - pr - q = 0.$$

Let's return to our consideration of recurrence relation (15). Since

$$r^2 - 12r + 20 = (r - 10)(r - 2),$$

the auxiliary equation in this case has solutions $r = 2$ and $r = 10$. This tells us that the only possibilities for geometric sequences satisfying recurrence relation (15) are those with closed forms $u_n = 2^n$ and $u_n = 10^n$. Note that these are the conjectures for sequences (i) and (ii) in Activity 28.

In fact, these two geometric sequences do satisfy recurrence relation (15), and, more generally, so does any sequence with a closed form

$$u_n = A \times 2^n + B \times 10^n, \tag{16}$$

where A and B are constants. To check this, let $u_0, u_1, u_2, \dots$ be a sequence with closed form (16), where A and B are constants. Then, for any $n = 2, 3, 4, \dots$,

$$u_{n-1} = A \times 2^{n-1} + B \times 10^{n-1}$$

and

$$u_{n-2} = A \times 2^{n-2} + B \times 10^{n-2},$$

so

$$\begin{aligned} 12u_{n-1} - 20u_{n-2} &= 12 \times A \times 2^{n-1} + 12 \times B \times 10^{n-1} \\ &\qquad - 20 \times A \times 2^{n-2} - 20 \times B \times 10^{n-2} \\ &= A(6 \times 2^n - 5 \times 2^n) + B(12 \times 10^{n-1} - 2 \times 10^{n-1}) \\ &= A \times 2^n + B \times 10 \times 10^{n-1} \\ &= u_n. \end{aligned}$$

This shows that the sequence satisfies recurrence relation (15).

In fact, it can be shown that *every* sequence that satisfies recurrence relation (15) has a closed form given by the formula

$$u_n = A \times 2^n + B \times 10^n, \tag{17}$$

where A and B are constants. In other words, equation (17) is the **general solution** of recurrence relation (15). The proof of this fact is beyond the scope of this unit.

The final step in solving a recurrence system that includes recurrence relation (15) is to take into account the values of the initial terms u_0 and u_1. Using these, you can find the values of the constants A and B for a particular recurrence sequence.

Let's try to come up with a closed form for sequence (iv) in Activity 28. In this case, $u_0 = 3$ and $u_1 = 22$, so we can substitute these values into the general solution of the recurrence relation to get two equations:

$$3 = A \times 2^0 + B \times 10^0; \quad \text{that is,} \quad 3 = A + B \tag{18}$$

$$22 = A \times 2^1 + B \times 10^1; \quad \text{that is,} \quad 22 = 2A + 10B. \tag{19}$$

This is a pair of simultaneous equations in two unknowns. To eliminate A, we can subtract two times equation (18) from equation (19), which gives

$$16 = 8B,$$

and hence $B = 2$. Substituting $B = 2$ into equation (18) then gives

$$3 = A + 2,$$

and hence $A = 1$. Thus a closed form for sequence (iv) is

$$u_n = 2^n + 2 \times 10^n \quad (n = 0, 1, 2, \ldots),$$

as conjectured in the solution to Activity 28.

The next activity introduces you to another type of example.

Activity 29 *Investigating a different type of recurrence system*

Consider the following recurrence relation:

$$u_n = 4u_{n-1} - 4u_{n-2} \quad (n = 2, 3, 4, \ldots).$$

(a) Write down and solve the auxiliary equation for this recurrence relation. What do you notice?

(b) In the table below, complete the columns u_2, u_3 and u_4 for each of the following pairs of initial terms.

	u_0	u_1	u_2	u_3	u_4
(i)	1	2			
(ii)	0	2			
(iii)	3	8			

(c) For $n = 0, 1, 2, 3, 4$, check that $u_n = 2^n$ in sequence (i) and that $u_n = n \times 2^n$ in sequence (ii).

(d) Check that the sequences given by $u_n = 2^n$ and $u_n = n \times 2^n$ satisfy the recurrence relation above, and show that any sequence given by

$$u_n = A \times 2^n + B \times n \times 2^n,$$

where A and B are constants, also satisfies it. Assuming that this formula gives a closed form for sequence (iii), can you work out the values of the constants A and B?

Activity 29 has shown you that, when the auxiliary equation for a second-order recurrence relation has only one solution, the formulas for closed forms of sequences satisfying the recurrence relation are rather more complicated than those that you've seen previously.

For the recurrence relation

$$u_n = 4u_{n-1} - 4u_{n-2} \quad (n = 2, 3, 4, \dots), \tag{20}$$

you found that, if A and B are constants, then any sequence with a closed form

$$u_n = A \times 2^n + B \times n \times 2^n, \tag{21}$$

satisfies the recurrence relation.

In fact, it can be shown that *every* sequence that satisfies recurrence relation (20) has a closed form given by equation (21). In other words, equation (21) is the **general solution** of this recurrence relation. The proof of this is beyond the scope of this unit. The general solution can be written slightly more neatly as

$$u_n = (A + Bn)2^n,$$

where A and B are constants.

As before, to find a closed form for a particular recurrence sequence, you can use the values of the initial terms u_0 and u_1 to find two simultaneous equations in the constants A and B. Solving these gives you the particular values of A and B for your sequence.

The following box summarises the two methods that you've seen for finding closed forms for second-order recurrence sequences. These methods cover the situations in which the auxiliary equation for the recurrence relation either has two distinct solutions or one (repeated) solution. Of course, there is a third possibility – the auxiliary equation may have no real solutions. In this situation, the general solution of the recurrence relation is considerably more complicated and can involve exponentials, sines and cosines. However, you won't encounter any recurrence relations of this type in this unit.

Strategy:
To find a closed form for a second-order recurrence sequence

Suppose that the sequence $u_0, u_1, u_2, \ldots$ is given by the recurrence system

$$u_0 = a, \quad u_1 = b, \quad u_n = pu_{n-1} + qu_{n-2} \quad (n = 2, 3, 4, \ldots).$$

To find a closed form for this sequence, proceed as follows.

1. Write down and solve the auxiliary equation for the recurrence relation, which is

   $$r^2 - pr - q = 0.$$

   There may be distinct real solutions, say $r = \alpha$ and $r = \beta$, or a single (repeated) real solution, say $r = \alpha$, or no real solutions.
2. Write down the general solution of the recurrence relation, using the table below, where A and B are constants.

Solutions of auxiliary equation	General solution
Distinct real solutions α, β	$u_n = A\alpha^n + B\beta^n$
Single real solution α	$u_n = (A + Bn)\alpha^n$
No real solutions	(not covered in MST125)

3. Find the values of A and B by using the values of the initial terms u_0 and u_1 to obtain two simultaneous equations in A and B and solving them.

Example 16 *Finding a closed form for a second-order recurrence sequence*

Use the strategy above to find a closed form for the sequence given by the recurrence system

$$u_0 = 4, \quad u_1 = 9, \quad u_n = 5u_{n-1} - 6u_{n-2} \quad (n = 2, 3, 4, \ldots).$$

Solution

Write down the auxiliary equation for the recurrence relation.

The auxiliary equation is

$$r^2 - 5r + 6 = 0.$$

Solve the auxiliary equation. In this case, the solutions can be found by factorising.

Since

$$r^2 - 5r + 6 = (r - 2)(r - 3),$$

the auxiliary equation has the solutions $r = 2$ and $r = 3$.

Write down the form of the general solution of the recurrence relation, using the table in step 2 of the strategy. In our case, there are two distinct real solutions of the auxiliary equation, $\alpha = 2$ and $\beta = 3$. Hence the form of the general solution is $u_n = A\alpha^n + B\beta^n$.

Thus the general solution of the recurrence relation is

$$u_n = A \times 2^n + B \times 3^n,$$

where A and B are constants.

Use the initial conditions to find two simultaneous equations in the unknowns A and B, and then solve these for A and B.

To find A and B, we use the initial terms of the sequence, $u_0 = 4$ and $u_1 = 9$. Substituting $n = 0$ and $u_0 = 4$ into the general solution, we obtain

$$4 = A \times 2^0 + B \times 3^0,$$

so

$$A + B = 4.$$

Similarly, substituting $n = 1$ and $u_1 = 9$ gives

$$9 = A \times 2^1 + B \times 3^1,$$

that is

$$2A + 3B = 9.$$

Subtracting twice the first equation from the second gives $B = 1$. Then, substituting this value of B in the first equation gives $A = 3$. Thus a closed form for the given recurrence sequence is

$$u_n = 3 \times 2^n + 3^n \quad (n = 0, 1, 2, \ldots).$$

Activity 30 *Finding closed forms for second-order recurrence sequences*

Use the strategy above to find closed forms for the sequences given by the following recurrence systems.

(a) $u_0 = 2, \quad u_1 = 7, \quad u_n = 7u_{n-1} - 12u_{n-2} \quad (n = 2, 3, 4, \ldots)$

(b) $u_0 = 2, \quad u_1 = 7, \quad u_n = 6u_{n-1} - 9u_{n-2} \quad (n = 2, 3, 4, \ldots)$

(c) $x_0 = 2, \quad x_1 = 7, \quad x_n = 2x_{n-1} + 8x_{n-2} \quad (n = 2, 3, 4, \ldots)$

(d) $a_0 = 1, \quad a_1 = 3, \quad a_n = -\frac{5}{2}a_{n-1} + \frac{3}{2}a_{n-2} \quad (n = 2, 3, 4, \ldots)$

Activity 31 *Solving recurrence systems using the computer*

Work through Section 9 of the *Computer algebra guide*, where you will learn how to use the computer algebra system to solve recurrence systems.

4.3 A closed form for the Fibonacci sequence

Since the Fibonacci sequence is defined by the linear second-order recurrence system

$$F_1 = 1, \quad F_2 = 1, \quad F_n = F_{n-1} + F_{n-2} \quad (n = 3, 4, 5, \ldots),$$

we can find a closed form for this sequence by using the strategy in the previous section.

The first step is to write down and solve the auxiliary equation of the recurrence relation, which is

$$r^2 - r - 1 = 0.$$

This equation can be solved using the quadratic formula, which gives

$$r = \frac{1 \pm \sqrt{1^2 - 4 \times 1 \times (-1)}}{2} = \frac{1 \pm \sqrt{5}}{2}.$$

The two solutions are therefore

$$\phi = \tfrac{1}{2}(1 + \sqrt{5}) = 1.618\ldots \quad \text{and} \quad \psi = \tfrac{1}{2}(1 - \sqrt{5}) = -0.618\ldots.$$

In the working that follows, we'll continue to denote these two solutions by ϕ and ψ, for brevity. The symbols ϕ and ψ are the lower-case Greek letters phi and psi, respectively.

The general solution of the recurrence relation is therefore

$$F_n = A\phi^n + B\psi^n,$$

where A and B are unknown constants. The values of these constants are determined by using the two initial terms of the sequence, $F_1 = 1$ and $F_2 = 1$. This gives us the simultaneous equations

$$A\phi + B\psi = 1$$
$$A\phi^2 + B\psi^2 = 1.$$

Now you *could* solve these, but to do so you would have to compute ϕ^2 and ψ^2, which is going to lead to rather a lot of algebraic manipulation. To make life easier, you can instead use the version of the recurrence system with the 0th term $F_0 = 0$:

$$F_0 = 0, \quad F_1 = 1, \quad F_n = F_{n-1} + F_{n-2} \quad (n = 2, 3, 4, \ldots).$$

This is still the same sequence, but with an extra term 0 at the beginning.

Substituting $n = 0$ and $F_0 = 0$ into the general solution, we obtain

$$0 = A\phi^0 + B\psi^0,$$

so

$$A + B = 0.$$

Similarly, substituting $n = 1$ and $F_1 = 1$ (as before) gives

$$1 = A\phi^1 + B\psi^1,$$

that is

$$A\phi + B\psi = 1.$$

Much better! On substituting $B = -A$ from the first equation into the second equation we obtain

$$A\phi - A\psi = 1,$$

which gives

$$A = \frac{1}{\phi - \psi}.$$

Now,

$$\phi - \psi = \frac{1+\sqrt{5}}{2} - \frac{1-\sqrt{5}}{2} = \frac{1+\sqrt{5}-1+\sqrt{5}}{2} = \sqrt{5}.$$

So

$$A = \frac{1}{\sqrt{5}}.$$

Thus $B = -A = -1/\sqrt{5}$, and the required closed form is

$$F_n = \frac{1}{\sqrt{5}}\phi^n - \frac{1}{\sqrt{5}}\psi^n = \frac{1}{\sqrt{5}}(\phi^n - \psi^n) \quad (n = 0, 1, 2, \ldots).$$

This remarkable formula for the Fibonacci sequence was first obtained in the early 18th century and was rediscovered in 1843 by JPM Binet, after whom it is named.

Jacques Philippe Marie Binet (1786–1856)

The formula is remarkable because it involves three *irrational* numbers, $\sqrt{5}, \phi$ and ψ, yet it gives an integer for every value of n.

Binet's formula

A closed form for the Fibonacci sequence is

$$F_n = \frac{1}{\sqrt{5}}(\phi^n - \psi^n) \quad (n = 0, 1, 2, \ldots),$$

where $\phi = \frac{1}{2}(1+\sqrt{5})$ and $\psi = \frac{1}{2}(1-\sqrt{5})$.

The number $\phi = \frac{1}{2}(1+\sqrt{5})$ is known as the **golden ratio**, for reasons explained in the following box.

The golden ratio

The number $\phi = \frac{1}{2}(1 + \sqrt{5})$ was known to the ancient Greeks since it arises in the solution of the following problem:

> Can a line AB be divided by a point P in such a way that the ratio of AB to AP is equal to the ratio of AP to PB?

It is easier to visualise ϕ as the aspect ratio (that is, the ratio of length to width) of a rectangle with the following property:

> If you cut the rectangle into a square and a smaller rectangle (as shown in Figure 10), then the smaller rectangle has the same aspect ratio as the original rectangle.

In fact, the number ϕ makes several appearances in geometric figures. As another example, consider a *regular pentagon*, that is, a pentagon with five equal sides and five equal angles. If the length of the sides of the regular pentagon is 1, then the length of each of its five diagonals is ϕ (see Figure 11). This fact was also known to the ancient Greeks.

In 1509, an Italian friar named Luca Pacioli (1445–1517) published an influential book called *De divina proportione* ('On the divine proportion'). This described many occurrences of the number ϕ in geometric figures, with fine illustrations thought to have been drawn by Pacioli's friend Leonardo da Vinci.

Martin Ohm (1792–1892), a German mathematician (and younger brother of the physicist Georg Ohm) is believed to have been the first person to use the term 'golden section' for ϕ. The modern term 'golden ratio' is derived from this. A rectangle with aspect ratio ϕ is called a *golden rectangle*.

There are many claims that the golden ratio has been used deliberately as an aesthetically pleasing proportion in the design of artefacts, for example in ancient Greek temples and sculptures. These claims should be treated with caution; some uses of the golden ratio are certainly deliberate, particularly following the publication of *De divina proportione*. Others, however, have probably arisen by coincidence, or are only approximate.

A modern example of the deliberate use of the golden ratio in art is in Salvador Dali's *The Sacrament of the Last Supper*, which is painted on a canvas whose dimensions are those of a golden rectangle, and which includes part of a huge dodecahedron (a three-dimensional solid whose faces are regular pentagons).

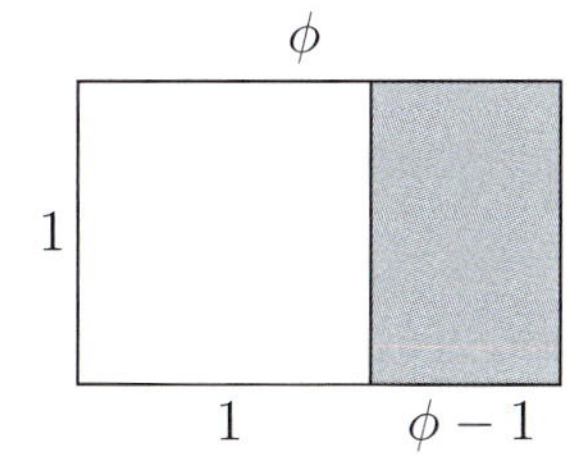

Figure 10 A rectangle with aspect ratio ϕ (a golden rectangle)

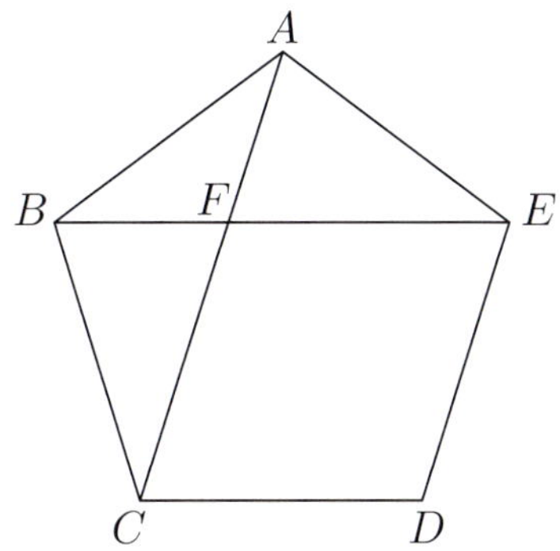

Figure 11 A regular pentagon. If AB has length 1, then AC has length ϕ, and AF has length $1/\phi$

The two terms ϕ^n and ψ^n that appear in Binet's formula have different long-term behaviour, that is, behaviour as n becomes very large. Since $\phi = 1.618\ldots$ is greater than 1, the geometric sequence (ϕ^n) tends to infinity as n tends to infinity. On the other hand, $\psi = -0.618\ldots$ lies between -1 and 0, so the sequence (ψ^n) alternates in sign and tends to 0 as n tends to infinity. For example, to three significant figures,

$$\begin{aligned}\psi &= -0.618,\\ \psi^2 &= 0.382,\\ \psi^3 &= -0.236,\\ &\vdots\\ \psi^{15} &= -7.33\times 10^{-4}.\end{aligned}$$

(The long-term behaviour of geometric sequences was covered in MST124 Unit 10.)

It is not feasible to use Binet's formula to find Fibonacci numbers by hand, other than for small integers n for which the values of F_n are already easy to find. However, the formula is suitable for finding Fibonacci numbers with a calculator, particularly if the following version is used.

Binet's approximation

F_n is the nearest integer to $\dfrac{\phi^n}{\sqrt{5}}$, for $n = 0, 1, 2, \ldots$.

To see why this fact holds, consider Binet's formula, which tells you that for $n = 0, 1, 2, \ldots$,

$$F_n = \frac{1}{\sqrt{5}}\phi^n - \frac{1}{\sqrt{5}}\psi^n.$$

The second term on the right, $-\psi^n/\sqrt{5}$, is always between $-\frac{1}{2}$ and $\frac{1}{2}$. This is because

$$\psi^n \text{ lies between } -1 \text{ and } 1,$$

and

$$\sqrt{5} = 2.236\ldots > 2.$$

Therefore, by Binet's formula,

$$F_n \text{ always lies within } \tfrac{1}{2} \text{ of } \frac{\phi^n}{\sqrt{5}}.$$

So, since F_n is an *integer*, it must be the nearest integer to $\phi^n/\sqrt{5}$.

For example, with $n = 15$, a calculator gives

$$\frac{\phi^{15}}{\sqrt{5}} = \frac{(\frac{1}{2}(1+\sqrt{5}))^{15}}{\sqrt{5}} = 609.999\,67 \text{ (to 5 d.p.)},$$

so

$$F_{15} = 610.$$

Activity 32 *Using Binet's approximation*

Use Binet's approximation to calculate F_{20}.

4.4 Finding second-order recurrence systems for counting problems

Now that you've seen how to find closed forms for some sequences specified by second-order recurrence systems, let's return to the task of finding recurrence systems to solve counting problems. As with the process of finding first-order recurrence systems in Section 3, the key step is to try to find a way of expressing the nth term in the sequence of answers to counting problems in terms of earlier terms in the sequence.

Example 17 *Counting tile arrangements using a second-order recurrence system*

A bathroom is to be redecorated to include a tiled border, 1 cm high and n cm wide. Three coloured tiles are available, as follows.

Red, measuring $1\,\text{cm} \times 1\,\text{cm}$:

Blue, measuring $1\,\text{cm} \times 2\,\text{cm}$:

Green, measuring $1\,\text{cm} \times 2\,\text{cm}$:

For example, here is a possible tiling of a strip 1 cm high and 8 cm wide:

Let u_n denote the number of ways to tile the $1\,\text{cm} \times n\,\text{cm}$ strip.

(a) Calculate u_n for each of $n = 1, 2, 3$.

(b) Find a recurrence system for the number of ways to tile the border.

(c) Using your recurrence system, find a closed form for the number of ways to tile the border.

Solution

(a) For $n = 1$, the only possible tiling is a single red tile, as shown below.

So $u_1 = 1$.

For $n = 2$, there are three possibilities:

So $u_2 = 3$.

For $n = 3$, there are five possibilities:

So $u_3 = 5$.

(b) To find a recurrence relation, try to divide up the problem by describing the object of size n in terms of objects of sizes $n - 1$ and $n - 2$.

Consider any $1\,\text{cm} \times n\,\text{cm}$ border. There are three possibilities for the last (rightmost) tile in the sequence:

If the last tile is red, we have

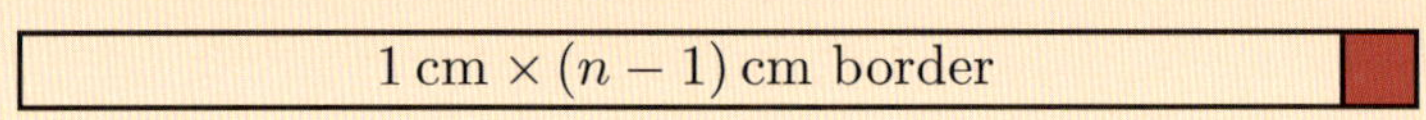

and there are u_{n-1} such tilings.

If the last tile is blue, then we have

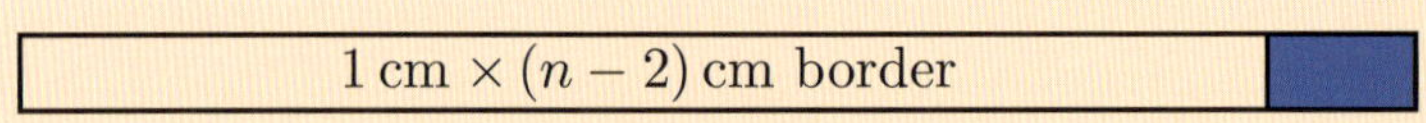

and there are u_{n-2} of these tilings.

Similarly, if the last tile is green, we have

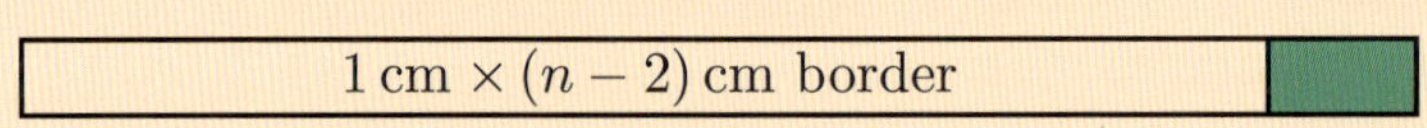

which again gives u_{n-2} tilings.

Use the addition principle to recombine the different cases.

Thus, by the addition principle, the number of tilings of a $1\,\text{cm} \times n\,\text{cm}$ border is

$$\begin{aligned} u_n &= u_{n-1} + u_{n-2} + u_{n-2} \\ &= u_{n-1} + 2u_{n-2}. \end{aligned}$$

Hence the sequence (u_n) satisfies the recurrence system

$$u_1 = 1, \quad u_2 = 3, \quad u_n = u_{n-1} + 2u_{n-2}, \quad (n = 3, 4, 5, \dots).$$

(c) Follow the strategy on page 79. First, write down and solve the auxiliary equation.

The auxiliary equation for the recurrence relation is

$$r^2 - r - 2 = 0.$$

Since $r^2 - r - 2 = (r+1)(r-2)$, the solutions to the auxiliary equation are $r = -1$ and $r = 2$.

Since the auxiliary equation has distinct real solutions $r = \alpha$ and $r = \beta$, the general solution to the recurrence relation is of the form $u_n = A\alpha^n + B\beta^n$.

Therefore the general solution to the recurrence relation is

$$u_n = A \times (-1)^n + B \times 2^n,$$

where A and B are constants.

When finding simultaneous equations to determine the constants, it can be easier to use the 0th and first terms of the sequence, rather than the first and second terms. To do this, we first need to find the 0th term, using the values for u_1 and u_2, together with the recurrence relation.

The first and second terms of the sequence are presently $u_1 = 1$ and $u_2 = 3$. To find the 0th term, rearrange the recurrence relation in the form

$$u_{n-2} = \tfrac{1}{2}(u_n - u_{n-1}).$$

Since $u_1 = 1$ and $u_2 = 3$, we find

$$u_0 = \tfrac{1}{2}(u_2 - u_1) = \tfrac{1}{2}(3 - 1) = 1.$$

To find A and B, we now use the initial terms of the sequence, $u_0 = 1$ and $u_1 = 1$. Substituting $n = 0$ and $u_0 = 1$ into the general solution, we obtain

$$1 = A \times (-1)^0 + B \times 2^0,$$

so

$$A + B = 1.$$

Similarly, substituting $n = 1$ and $u_1 = 1$ gives

$$1 = A \times (-1)^1 + B \times 2^1,$$

that is

$$-A + 2B = 1.$$

Adding the first equation to the second gives $3B = 2$, so $B = \frac{2}{3}$. Substituting this value of B in the first equation then gives $A = \frac{1}{3}$. Thus the number of tilings of a $1\,\text{cm} \times n\,\text{cm}$ strip is given by

$$u_n = \tfrac{1}{3} \times (-1)^n + \tfrac{2}{3} \times 2^n \quad (n = 1, 2, \ldots).$$

Calculating the 0th term in the example above does not in fact simplify the algebra very much, but is more worthwhile for some recurrence systems.

It is worth taking a moment to consider the 0th term in the example above: does $u_0 = 1$ make sense in the context of the question? If you are prepared to accept that there is exactly one tiling of a $1\,\text{cm} \times 0\,\text{cm}$ non-existent strip, then yes! However, you might equally think that there can be no tilings of an empty strip. So, although it is mathematically acceptable to use the 0th term to simplify the simultaneous equations, it does not always make sense in the context of the original problem.

The strategy for finding a second-order recurrence system for a sequence of counting problems is much the same as the strategy for finding first-order recurrence systems given on page 65. However, because second-order recurrence relations involve the two preceding terms, you should expect the reasoning to be a little more complicated.

Here is one for you to try.

Activity 33 *Counting sequences with no repeated letter A*

Let u_n denote the number of sequences of length n made up of the letters A and B that contain no consecutive occurrences of the letter A.

(a) Find the first two terms of the sequence, u_1 and u_2.

(b) Show that u_n satisfies the Fibonacci recurrence relation,

$$u_n = u_{n-1} + u_{n-2}.$$

(c) Hence find the number of sequences of length 10 that contain no consecutive occurrences of the letter A.

Learning outcomes

After studying this unit, you should be able to:

- apply the multiplication principle, addition principle and subtraction principle to counting problems
- apply the counting principles together to solve counting problems
- use the formulas for the number of k-element sequences of n objects, the number of permutations of n objects taken k at a time and the number of combinations of n objects taken k at a time
- calculate probabilities by counting elements in appropriate sample spaces and events
- find closed forms for certain first- and second-order recurrence sequences
- find first- and second-order recurrence systems for counting problems
- understand the Fibonacci sequence, Binet's formula and Binet's approximation.

Closing remarks

Well done for reaching the end of MST125!

We hope that you have enjoyed the challenge of exploring some new ideas in both pure and applied mathematics, and have been inspired by both the beauty and the power of mathematical thinking. You should now be well equipped to study mathematics at Level 2 and develop further as a mathematician, or alternatively to apply mathematics to other subject areas such as science, engineering and economics.

By studying MST125, you'll have extended your knowledge of mathematics and your ability to use it to solve problems. You've seen how combining different mathematical ideas can lead to new and powerful techniques. For example, you used ideas about vectors and matrices together to work with geometric transformations and also to learn about eigenvalues and eigenvectors, which provide a key to solving problems in many different areas. And you used vectors and calculus together to solve problems involving motion in two and three dimensions.

You've also extended many of the skills that you learned in MST124. For instance, you've now learned many more techniques for integrating functions, and techniques for solving differential equations. You've also developed skills in using calculus practically, for example, to determine the shape of curves or to model physical situations. And you have strengthened your general mathematical understanding by learning how to rigorously prove mathematical results. This is an essential part of mathematics, especially pure mathematics, at higher levels.

However there's more to MST125 than just developing new skills! We hope that you have appreciated the beauty of some of the results from pure mathematics that you've met, such as Fermat's little theorem or the fact that circles, parabolas, ellipses and hyperbolas are all examples of the same type of curve, with simple methods of construction. Or perhaps you've been impressed with how you can apply mathematics to solve some real-world problems, such as those involving forces, and the motion that results from forces. Or even been inspired by how differential equations can give you powerful insights into problems that involve rates of change and help you to interpret seemingly complicated situations as much simpler systems. Remember too that many topics from pure mathematics also have applications in the real world – for example, you saw how number theory is used in ISBN numbers, how combinatorics is used to calculate probabilities, and how geometric transformations can be used to manipulate shapes, a technique that has applications in computer graphics, for example.

The MST125 team hopes that you have enjoyed your journey through MST125 and that you will continue to enjoy applying the mathematics that you have learned to your chosen field.

Solutions to activities

Solution to Activity 1

There is one vegetarian starter option (camembert), two mains (pasta and omelette) and two desserts (tart and bun). The tree diagram is:

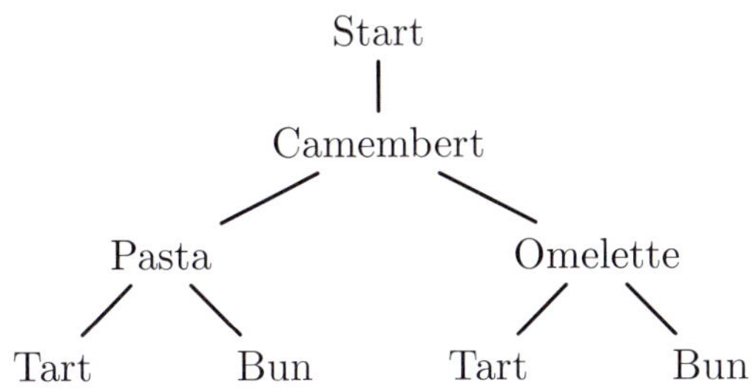

There are four paths from the top of the tree diagram to the bottom, so there are four different vegetarian three-course meals. These are:

Camembert, Pasta, Tart
Camembert, Pasta, Bun
Camembert, Omelette, Tart
Camembert, Omelette, Bun

(Your tree diagram will look different if you chose your courses in a different order.)

Solution to Activity 2

(a) The woman has to make four successive decisions, about which hat, coat, gloves and boots to wear. There are two possible hats, three possible coats, four possible pairs of gloves and two possible pairs of boots.

We can use the multiplication principle because the number of options for each item of clothing is fixed. Hence the number of ways the woman can dress for her winter walk is

$$2 \times 3 \times 4 \times 2 = 48.$$

(b) A person taking the multiple choice test has to answer ten questions, each of which involves a choice between a number of possible answers, so there are ten successive choices to be made. The answers to the first five questions have to be selected from four possible options, and the answers to the next five questions have to be selected from six possible options.

We can use the multiplication principle because the number of possible answers to each question is fixed (four for each of the first five questions, and six for each of the next five). Therefore the total number of ways to answer the test is

$$\begin{aligned} &4 \times 4 \times 4 \times 4 \times 4 \times 6 \times 6 \times 6 \times 6 \times 6 \\ &\quad = 4^5 \times 6^5 = 7\,962\,624. \end{aligned}$$

(c) To construct a password, you must choose one of the numbers $0, 1, \dots, 9$ for the first character, and then one of the 26 upper-case letters of the alphabet for each of the remaining six characters. Thus there are seven successive choices to be made in all.

We can use the multiplication principle because the number of options for each character of the password is fixed: the ten possible numbers $0, 1, \dots, 9$ for the first character, and the 26 possible letters $A, B, \dots, Z$ for each of the remaining six characters. Thus the number of possible passwords is

$$\begin{aligned} &10 \times 26 \times 26 \times 26 \times 26 \times 26 \times 26 \\ &\quad = 10 \times 26^6 = 3\,089\,157\,760. \end{aligned}$$

Solution to Activity 3

(a) The set $\{1, 2\}$ has four subsets:

$$\varnothing \ \{1\} \ \{2\} \ \{1,2\}.$$

(b) The set $\{1, 2, 3\}$ has eight subsets:

$$\varnothing \ \{1\} \ \{2\} \ \{3\} \ \{1,2\} \ \{1,3\} \ \{2,3\} \ \{1,2,3\}.$$

Solution to Activity 4

(a) (i) There are 4 subsets that do not contain the element 1, but do contain the element 2, namely:

$$\{2\} \ \{2,3\} \ \{2,4\} \ \{2,3,4\}.$$

(ii) There are 8 subsets that contain either the element 1 or the element 2, but not both, namely:

$$\{1\} \ \{1,3\} \ \{1,4\} \ \{1,3,4\},$$
$$\{2\} \ \{2,3\} \ \{2,4\} \ \{2,3,4\}.$$

(b) (i) The condition 'do not contain the element 1, but do contain the element 2' means that every subset of X of the required form consists of the element 2, followed by any subset of $\{3, 4, 5, \dots, n\}$.

So we need to choose a subset of $\{3, 4, 5, \ldots, n\}$. Since $\{3, 4, 5, \ldots, n\}$ contains $n - 2$ elements, it has 2^{n-2} subsets.

Therefore there are 2^{n-2} subsets of X containing the element 2 but not the element 1.

(ii) Every subset of the required form consists of either the element 1 or the element 2, together with a subset of $\{3, 4, 5, \ldots, n\}$. So there are two choices to be made.

First, choose whether the subset contains the element 1 or the element 2. There are two options for this choice.

Second, choose any subset of $\{3, 4, 5, \ldots, n\}$. As seen in the solution to part (a), there are 2^{n-2} such subsets, so there are 2^{n-2} options for this choice.

Since the number of options for each choice is fixed, we can use the multiplication principle. It follows that the number of subsets of X that contain either the element 1 or the element 2, but not both, is $2 \times 2^{n-2} = 2^{n-1}$.

Solution to Activity 5

(a) The subsets we want to count must include all the odd numbers in X. Therefore, if we split X into two parts, one containing just the odd numbers from X and the other containing just the even numbers from X, it follows that we can form a subset of the type we want by combining the whole of the part containing just the odd numbers with any subset of the part containing just the even numbers. In other words, the number of subsets of X containing all the odd numbers in X is equal to the number of subsets of the part of X containing just the even numbers.

When n is even, it is divisible by 2, so $n = 2k$ for some positive integer k. Hence there are k even numbers in X, and the number of subsets of the part of X containing just the even numbers is $2^k = 2^{n/2}$. As we have just argued, this is the same as the number of subsets of X containing all of the odd numbers in X.

(b) By the same reasoning as in part (a), we split X into two parts, one containing just the odd numbers from X and the other containing just the even numbers from X. We then count the number of subsets of the part of X containing just the even numbers.

Since n is odd, $n = 2k + 1$ for some integer $k \geq 0$, so there are k even numbers (and $k + 1$ odd numbers) in X. Thus, there are $2^k = 2^{(n-1)/2}$ subsets of X containing all the odd numbers in X.

(Notice in particular that this is still true when $k = 0$. For then, $n = 1$ and $X = \{1\}$, so there is just $2^0 = 1$ subset of X containing all of the odd numbers in X.)

Solution to Activity 6

(a) There are two possible starters and three possible main courses, so by the multiplication principle there are $2 \times 3 = 6$ possible two-course meals consisting of a starter and a main.

(b) There are three possible main courses and two possible desserts, so by the multiplication principle there are $3 \times 2 = 6$ possible two-course meals consisting of a main course and a dessert.

Solution to Activity 7

(a) $\{2, 4, 6\} \cap \{1, 3, 5\} = \varnothing$, so the sets in this collection are pairwise disjoint.

(b) Although $\{1, 3\} \cap \{2, 4\} = \varnothing$, we find that $\{1, 3\} \cap \{1, 2\} = \{1\}$ is not empty, so the sets in this collection are not pairwise disjoint.

(c) Each of the seven dishes offered at the café appears exactly once. Therefore the intersections are all empty:

$$\{\text{pasta, camembert, tart}\} \cap \{\text{bun, salad}\} = \varnothing,$$
$$\{\text{pasta, camembert, tart}\} \cap \{\text{paté, omelette}\} = \varnothing,$$
$$\{\text{bun, salad}\} \cap \{\text{paté, omelette}\} = \varnothing,$$

so the sets in this collection are pairwise disjoint.

(d) The intersection

$$\{\text{paté, omelette}\} \cap \{\text{paté, salad}\} = \{\text{paté}\}$$

is not empty, so the sets in the given collection are not pairwise disjoint.

Solution to Activity 8

(a) The set we want to count is the set of all possible pairs of books in different languages. Call this set S.

Define the following three subsets:

$S_1 = \{\text{Spanish/French pairs of books}\}$

$S_2 = \{\text{Spanish/Italian pairs of books}\}$

$S_3 = \{\text{French/Italian pairs of books}\}$.

These three subsets are pairwise disjoint, and their union is equal to S.

By the multiplication principle, the number of Spanish/French pairs of books is $|S_1| = 5 \times 6 = 30$. Similarly, the number of Spanish/Italian pairs of books is $|S_2| = 5 \times 8 = 40$, again by the multiplication principle. Finally, the number of French/Italian pairs of books is $|S_3| = 6 \times 8 = 48$.

Hence, by the addition principle, $|S| = 30 + 40 + 48 = 118$, which is the number of ways of choosing two books in different languages.

(b) The set we want to count is the set of all possible access codes. Call this set S.

Since an access code can consist of four, five or six digits, we can split S into subsets containing all possible access codes of each of these three lengths.

Let

$S_1 = \{\text{4-digit access codes}\}$

$S_2 = \{\text{5-digit access codes}\}$

$S_3 = \{\text{6-digit access codes}\}$.

These three subsets are pairwise disjoint, and their union is equal to S.

Each access code in S_1 consists of four digits selected from the numbers $0, 1, \ldots, 9$, so there are four choices to make between 10 possible digits. By the multiplication principle, it follows that

$$|S_1| = 10 \times 10 \times 10 \times 10 = 10^4 = 10\,000.$$

Similarly,

$$|S_2| = 10^5 = 100\,000,$$

and

$$|S_3| = 10^6 = 1\,000\,000.$$

Hence, by the addition principle, the total number of possible access codes is $|S| = 10\,000 + 100\,000 + 1\,000\,000 = 1\,110\,000$.

(c) The set to be counted is the set of all positive integers less than 1000 that do not contain any of the odd digits $1, 3, 5, 7$ or 9 in their decimal representations. Call this set S.

Divide the problem into cases, depending on how many digits there are in an element of S. Let

$S_1 = \{\text{1-digit numbers in } S\}$

$S_2 = \{\text{2-digit numbers in } S\}$

$S_3 = \{\text{3-digit numbers in } S\}$.

These subsets are pairwise disjoint and their union is S. Hence it follows from the addition principle that

$$|S| = |S_1| + |S_2| + |S_3|.$$

Since we are considering only positive integers, $S_1 = \{2, 4, 6, 8\}$, and therefore $|S_1| = 4$.

Consider a number in S_2. The tens digit of this number cannot be 0 or any of the odd digits, so it must be one of the four numbers 2, 4, 6, or 8. The units digit can be 0, or one of 2, 4, 6, or 8, so there are five options for this choice. Hence, by the multiplication principle,

$$|S_2| = 4 \times 5 = 20.$$

Now consider a number in S_3. There are 4 options for the hundreds digit, and 5 options each for the tens and units digits. Hence, by the multiplication principle,

$$|S_3| = 4 \times 5 \times 5 = 100.$$

Therefore it follows by the addition principle that the number of positive integers less than 1000 that do not contain any odd digits in their decimal representations is

$$4 + 20 + 100 = 124.$$

(Alternatively, you can solve this problem by using a similar method to that used in the alternative solution to Example 4, given on page 22. In this method, you treat every number less than 1000 as consisting of 3 digits, by adding leading 0s. The possible options for each digit are then any of the five numbers $0, 2, 4, 6$ or 8. However, since you are asked to count only *positive* integers less than 1000, you must exclude the number '000' = 0. It then follows by the multiplication principle that the number of positive integers less than 1000 that do not contain any odd digits in their decimal representations is

$$5^3 - 1 = 125 - 1 = 124,$$

as before.)

Solution to Activity 9

(a) We need to count the set S of all positive integers less than 1000 that contain at least one odd digit in their decimal representations.

Let $U = \{1, 2, \dots, 999\}$. Then $|U| = 999$, and S is a subset of U. Since every number in U either contains at least one odd digit, or contains no odd digits, we conclude that the complement of S in U is the set $\overline{S}$ consisting of all positive integers less than 1000 that contain no odd digits in their decimal representations.

By the solution to Activity 8(c), we know that $|\overline{S}| = 124$. Therefore, by the subtraction principle,

$$|S| = |U| - |\overline{S}| = 999 - 124 = 875.$$

Hence there are 875 positive integers less than 1000 with at least one odd digit in their decimal representations.

(b) (i) There are 26 ways to pick each of the four letters. Thus, by the multiplication principle, the number of possible words is

$$26 \times 26 \times 26 \times 26 = 26^4 = 456\,976.$$

(ii) The number of words containing no vowels is equal to the number of words containing only consonants. There are 5 vowels and therefore $26 - 5 = 21$ consonants, so by the multiplication principle there are $21^4 = 194\,481$ possible words that contain no vowels.

(iii) We use the subtraction principle. Let U be the set of all possible words consisting of four letters, each selected from the 26 upper-case letters $A, B, C, \dots, Z$. We want to count the set S consisting of all such words that contain at least one vowel. The complement of S in U is therefore the set $\overline{S}$ of all words containing no vowels.

From part (i), we know that $|U| = 456\,976$, and from part (ii) we know that $|\overline{S}| = 194\,481$.

Therefore by the subtraction principle we have

$$|S| = |U| - |\overline{S}| = 456\,976 - 194\,481 = 262\,495.$$

Hence there are 262 495 possible words that contain at least one vowel.

(c) (i) To choose the pieces of fruit for the basket, we make three successive choices: one to choose the number of apples, one for the number of oranges, and one for the number of pears.

There are 6 apples, so we can put 0, 1, 2, 3, 4, 5 or 6 apples into the basket. Thus, there are 7 options for the number of apples we put into the basket.

Similarly, there are 5 oranges, so we can put 0, 1, 2, 3, 4 or 5 oranges into the basket, giving 6 options.

Finally, we can put 0, 1, 2 or 3 pears into the basket, giving 4 options.

Thus, by the multiplication principle there are

$$7 \times 6 \times 4 = 168$$

possible different baskets of fruit.

(Note that choosing 0 apples, 0 oranges and 0 pears is allowed, so the 'empty' basket has been included in this count.)

(ii) We use the subtraction principle. Let U be the set of all possible baskets of fruit. From part (i), we know that $|U| = 168$. We want to count the set S consisting of all such baskets that contain at least one piece of fruit. The complement of S in U is the set $\overline{S}$ which consists of the one possible basket that contains no fruit. In other words, we have $|\overline{S}| = 1$. Therefore, by the subtraction principle there are

$$|S| = |U| - |\overline{S}| = 168 - 1 = 167$$

different non-empty baskets of fruit.

(iii) We again use the subtraction principle. Let U be the set of all possible baskets of fruit. From part (i), we know that $|U| = 168$. We want to count the set S consisting of all such baskets that contain at least two pieces of fruit. The complement of S in U is the set $\overline{S}$ which contains the basket with no fruit, and any basket containing just one piece of fruit.

We already know from part (ii) that there is just one empty basket. Furthermore, there are three possible baskets containing exactly one piece of fruit, since this piece of fruit can be an apple, an orange, or a pear. Therefore, there are

$$|\overline{S}| = 3 + 1 = 4,$$

possible baskets with 0 or 1 pieces of fruit.

Finally, by the subtraction principle, there are

$$|S| = |U| - |\overline{S}| = 168 - 4 = 164$$

different baskets of fruit with at least two pieces of fruit.

Solution to Activity 10

(a) We want to count the positive integers whose decimal representations consist of two digits, with no digits repeated.

The first digit of any such integer can be any of the digits $1, 2, 3, \ldots, 9$, so there are nine possible options for the first digit. The second digit can be any of the digits $0, 1, 2, \ldots, 9$ except the digit chosen for the first digit, so there are also nine possible options for the second digit, no matter what the first digit is. Hence, by the multiplication principle, the number of positive integers whose decimal representations consist of two digits, with no digits repeated, is $9 \times 9 = 81$.

(Alternatively, you can solve this problem using the subtraction principle. Let S be the set of integers that we want to count, and let U be the set of all positive integers between 10 and 99 inclusive. Then

$$|S| = |U| - |\overline{S}|$$

where $\overline{S}$ is the set of all integers between 10 and 99 inclusive that do have a repeated digit.

First, let's count $|U|$. There are 99 numbers between 1 and 99 inclusive, of which the first 9 are smaller than 10, so, by the subtraction principle,

$$|U| = 99 - 9 = 90.$$

Next,

$$\overline{S} = \{11, 22, 33, 44, 55, 66, 77, 88, 99\},$$

so $|\overline{S}| = 9$. Hence the number of two-digit positive integers with no digits repeated is

$$|S| = 90 - 9 = 81.)$$

(b) First consider a palindrome of length n, where n is even. Then $n = 2k$ for some positive integer k.

Since a palindrome reads the same both forwards and backwards, a palindrome of even length is completely determined by the choices of letters in the first half of the word. Thus, in a palindrome of length $n = 2k$, each of the first k letters can be any of $A, B, \ldots, Z$, and the remaining k letters then repeat these selected letters in the reverse order. In other words, there are 26 possible options for each of the first k letters, and only 1 option for each of the remaining k letters.

Hence, by the multiplication principle, the number of palindromes of length n when $n = 2k$ is even is given by

$$26^k \times 1^k = 26^{n/2}.$$

Now consider a palindrome of length n, where n is odd. Then $n = 2k + 1$ for some non-negative integer k.

A palindrome of odd length $n = 2k + 1$ is completely determined by the choices of the first $k + 1$ letters, and the remaining k letters then repeat the first k letters selected, but in the reverse order. Hence there are 26 possible options for each of the first $k + 1$ letters, and only 1 option for each of the remaining k letters.

Thus, by the multiplication principle, the number of palindromes of length n when $n = 2k + 1$ is odd is given by

$$26^{k+1} \times 1^k = 26^{(n+1)/2}.$$

(c) Consider a two-digit positive integer where the first digit is greater than the second digit. The first digit can be any of the numbers $1, 2, 3, \dots, 9$. However, the number of options for the second digit depends on the choice of the first digit, so we cannot use the multiplication principle.

Suppose the first digit is 9. Then the second digit can be any of the numbers $0, 1, 2, \dots, 8$, so there are nine possible options.

Now suppose the first digit is 8. Then the second digit can be any of the numbers $0, 1, 2, \dots, 7$, so there are eight possible options.

Similarly, if the first digit is 7, there are seven possible options for the second digit, if the first digit is 6, there are six possible options for the second digit, and so on. Finally, if the first digit is 1, there is only one possible option for the second digit, namely 0.

Since the first digit must be one of the numbers $1, 2, 3, \dots, 9$, we can apply the addition principle and conclude that the number of two digit positive integers where the first digit is greater than the second digit is

$$9 + 8 + 7 + 6 + 5 + 4 + 3 + 2 + 1 = 45.$$

(d) We want to count the elements in the set of all possible access codes, that is, the set of all four-character codes where each character is selected either from the numbers $0, 1, \dots, 9$, or from the letters $A, B, \dots, Z$, but where at most one of the first two characters is a letter. Call this set S.

We can divide up S into two disjoint subsets, according to whether or not the first character is a letter, as follows:

S_1 = set of all access codes where the first character is a letter,

S_2 = set of all access codes where the first character is a number.

Consider an element of S_1. The first character is a letter, so there are 26 possible options. The second character cannot be another letter, because at most one of the first two characters can be a letter, so it must be a number. Hence there are 10 possible options for the second character. Each of the third and fourth characters can be either a letter or a number, so there are 36 possible options. Hence, by the multiplication principle,

$$|S_1| = 26 \times 10 \times 36 \times 36 = 336\,960.$$

Now consider an element of S_2. The first character is a number, so there are 10 possible options. The second character can be either a letter or a number, so there are 36 possible options. Similarly, there are 36 possible options for each of the third and fourth characters. Hence, by the multiplication principle,

$$|S_2| = 10 \times 36 \times 36 \times 36 = 466\,560.$$

Since S_1 and S_2 are disjoint and their union is S, we can combine these results using the addition principle, and conclude that the number of possible access codes to the safety deposit box is

$$|S| = |S_1| + |S_2| = 336\,960 + 466\,560 = 803\,520.$$

(Alternatively, you could solve this problem using the subtraction principle. Let U be the set of all four-character codes, where each character can be either a letter or a number. Then the complement $\overline{S}$ of S in U is the number of such codes where both of the first two characters are letters. By the multiplication principle, we have

$$|U| = 36^4 = 1\,679\,616,$$

and

$$|\overline{S}| = 26 \times 26 \times 36 \times 36 = 876\,096.$$

Hence, by the subtraction principle,

$$|S| = |U| - |\overline{S}| = 1\,679\,616 - 876\,096 = 803\,520,$$

as before.)

Solution to Activity 11

(a) There are 26 letters in the alphabet, and each letter in a two-letter sequence can be any of these 26 letters because repetitions are allowed. Hence, by the multiplication principle, there are $26 \times 26 = 676$ possible two-letter sequences.

(b) As in (a), each of the three letters in the sequence can be any of the 26 letters $A, B, C, \dots, Z$, so by the multiplication principle there are $26 \times 26 \times 26 = 17\,576$ possible three-letter sequences.

(c) Each of the k letters in the sequence can be any one of the 26 upper-case letters in the alphabet.

Therefore, by the multiplication principle, the number of possible k-letter sequences is

$$\underbrace{26 \times 26 \times \cdots \times 26}_{k \text{ times}} = 26^k.$$

Solution to Activity 12

The six three-letter permutations are

$$ABC, \quad BAC, \quad CAB,$$
$$ACB, \quad BCA, \quad CBA.$$

Solution to Activity 13

Medals are awarded to 3 competitors out of 16, and the order of the three competitors is important since different types of medals are awarded for first, second and third place. Therefore we need to count the number of permutations of 16 objects taken 3 at a time, so there are

$$^{16}P_3 = 16 \times 15 \times 14 = 3360$$

ways to award the medals.

Solution to Activity 14

There are 6 dishes on the tapas menu. Three different dishes need to be chosen, and the order of these dishes does not matter. Therefore, the number of possible meals made up of three dishes is

$$^{6}C_3 = \frac{6 \times 5 \times 4}{3 \times 2 \times 1} = 20.$$

Solution to Activity 15

(a) It is reasonable to assume that the order in which the team is selected does not matter. However, all 6 members of the team must obviously be distinct, so repetitions are not allowed. Therefore, the number of teams is equal to the number of combinations of 15 students taken 6 at a time, which is

$$^{15}C_6 = \frac{15 \times 14 \times 13 \times 12 \times 11 \times 10}{6 \times 5 \times 4 \times 3 \times 2 \times 1} = 5005.$$

Therefore there are 5005 possible teams.

(b) For a prize list, the order of the students matters. Also, repetitions are not allowed, since for example a student cannot simultaneously come first and fourth! Therefore, the number of possible prize lists is equal to the number of permutations of 15 students taken 5 at a time. This is

$$^{15}P_5 = 15 \times 14 \times 13 \times 12 \times 11 = 360\,360.$$

Therefore there are 360 360 possible prize lists.

(c) The order in which students are listed is important, because we want to know which student came top in which exam. However, repetitions are allowed: it is quite possible that a student could come top in more than one exam. Therefore, the number of lists is equal to the number of 3-element sequences of the 15 students. This is

$$15^3 = 3375.$$

Therefore, there are 3375 possible lists of students.

Solution to Activity 16

(a) Each team can be chosen by first choosing the two junior employees and then choosing the two senior employees. The order in which the employees are chosen does not matter.

The number of ways to choose the two junior employees is $^{4}C_2 = 6$.

The number of ways to choose the two senior employees is $^{3}C_2 = 3$.

Hence, by the multiplication principle, the total number of ways to choose the team is $6 \times 3 = 18$.

(b) To choose each possible team of six children, we can first decide how many boys and how many girls will be in the team. The possibilities are two boys and four girls, three boys and three girls, and four boys and two girls. Then for each possibility we can decide which particular boys and girls will be in the team. The order in which the children are selected does not matter.

First consider a team composed of two boys and four girls. The number of ways to choose the two boys is $^{14}C_2$, and the number of ways to choose the four girls is $^{12}C_4$. So, by the multiplication principle, the total number of ways to choose the team in this case is

$$^{14}C_2 \times {}^{12}C_4 = 91 \times 495 = 45\,045.$$

Similarly, the number of ways to choose a team of three boys and three girls is

$$^{14}C_3 \times {}^{12}C_3 = 364 \times 220 = 80\,080,$$

and the number of ways to choose a team of four boys and two girls is

$$^{14}C_4 \times {}^{12}C_2 = 1001 \times 66 = 66\,066.$$

Therefore, by the addition principle, the total number of ways to choose the team is

$$\begin{aligned} &{}^{14}C_2 \times {}^{12}C_4 + {}^{14}C_3 \times {}^{12}C_3 + {}^{14}C_4 \times {}^{12}C_2 \\ &= 45\,045 + 80\,080 + 66\,066 \\ &= 191\,191. \end{aligned}$$

(c) (i) In choosing an integer of the type described, the order in which the digits are selected is important. So the total number of integers of the type described is $^6P_4 = 360$.

(ii) To choose one of the integers that is larger than 6000, we can first write down the 6, then a permutation of 3 digits from the five digits 1, 2, 3, 4, 5. So the number of such integers is $^5P_3 = 60$.

(iii) To choose one of the integers that is larger than 5000, we can first write down a 5 or a 6, then a permutation of 3 digits from the remaining five digits. There are 2 ways to choose either a 5 or a 6, and then $^5P_3 = 60$ ways to choose the permutation of 3 digits from 5. So, by the multiplication principle, the number of such integers that are larger than 5000 is $2 \times 60 = 120$.

(iv) By the subtraction principle, the number of such integers smaller than 5000 is equal to the total number of integers of the type described minus the number that are larger than 5000. So the required answer is $360 - 120 = 240$.

(Alternatively, to choose one of the integers that is smaller than 5000, we can first write down one of the digits 1, 2, 3 or 4, then a permutation of 3 digits from the remaining five digits. So, by the multiplication principle, the number of such integers smaller than 5000 is $4 \times 60 = 240$.)

Solution to Activity 17

(a) The sample space S can be taken to comprise all five-letter sequences made up of the letters H and T. For example, $HHHHH$ corresponds to the coin showing heads every time.

By the formula for the number of k-letter sequences from n objects, we deduce that there are $2^5 = 32$ possible sequences. Thus the size of the sample space S is 32.

The event is $E = \{HHHHH\}$. Therefore the probability that the coin lands showing heads every time is

$$P(E) = \tfrac{1}{32}.$$

(b) The sample space S is the same as in part (a). The size of the event E that at least one toss of the coin shows heads can be calculated using the subtraction principle. Consider the event $\overline{E}$ that is the complement of E. This consists of all outcomes in S such that *no* toss of the coin shows heads, which is the same as saying that all five tosses show tails.

So $\overline{E} = \{TTTTT\}$. Since E and $\overline{E}$ are disjoint and since $E \cup \overline{E} = S$, by the subtraction principle we have

$$|E| = |S| - |\overline{E}| = 32 - 1 = 31.$$

Therefore the probability that at least one toss of the coin shows heads is

$$P(E) = \tfrac{31}{32}.$$

(c) The sample space S is the same as in part (a). The event E consists of the following outcomes,

$$E = \{HTTTT, THTTT, TTHTT, TTTHT, TTTTH\}.$$

By inspection, we see that $|E| = 5$, and therefore the probability that exactly one toss of the coin shows heads is

$$P(E) = \tfrac{5}{32}.$$

(d) The sample space S is the same as in part (a). In part (b), it was found that 31 outcomes included at least one head. In part (c), it was found that there are 5 outcomes with exactly one head. We can count the size of the event E that there are at least two heads by taking the 31 outcomes from part (b), and subtracting the 5 outcomes from part (c).

Thus, E contains $31 - 5 = 26$ outcomes, by the subtraction principle. Therefore the probability that at least two tosses of the coin show heads is

$$P(E) = \frac{26}{32} = \frac{13}{16}.$$

(There are several ways to calculate the probabilities in this activity. For example, you could list all 32 elements of the sample space. The solutions shown here illustrate how the subtraction principle can be used to avoid listing too many elements, and how to make use of answers that you have already found.)

Solution to Activity 18

The sample space S consists of the ${}^{49}C_6 = 13\,983\,816$ different ways to draw the 6 winning numbers. Throughout, we view the numbers on the player's ticket as fixed.

The event E of not winning a prize, which is a subset of S, can be divided into the following three disjoint subsets:

E_0 = all combinations of 6 numbers matching 0 numbers on the ticket

E_1 = all combinations of 6 numbers matching 1 number on the ticket

E_2 = all combinations of 6 numbers matching 2 numbers on the ticket

The event E_0 consists of combinations of 6 numbers chosen from the 43 numbers that are not on the ticket. Therefore

$$|E_0| = {}^{43}C_6 = 6\,096\,454.$$

The event E_1 consists of combinations of 6 numbers where one of them matches a number on the ticket, and the remaining 5 come from the 43 numbers not on the ticket. Therefore, by the multiplication principle,

$$|E_1| = {}^{6}C_1 \times {}^{43}C_5 = 6 \times 962\,598 = 5\,775\,588.$$

The event E_2 consists of combinations of 6 numbers where two of them match numbers on the ticket, and the remaining 4 come from the 43 numbers not on the ticket. Therefore, by the multiplication principle,

$$|E_2| = {}^{6}C_2 \times {}^{43}C_4 = 15 \times 123\,410 = 1\,851\,150.$$

Now, by the addition principle,

$$\begin{aligned}|E| &= |E_0| + |E_1| + |E_2| \\ &= 6\,096\,454 + 5\,775\,588 + 1\,851\,150 \\ &= 13\,723\,192,\end{aligned}$$

so the probability of not winning a prize is

$$\frac{|E|}{|S|} = \frac{13\,723\,192}{13\,983\,816} = 0.981 \text{ (to 3 s.f.)}.$$

(You can also calculate the probability of not winning a prize using the subtraction principle. From Example 11, you know the probability of matching all 6 numbers, and the probability of matching exactly 3. Next, use a similar method to calculate the sizes of E_4 and E_5, which are the events where exactly 4 and exactly 5 of the numbers are matched, respectively. You can then subtract the number of outcomes matching 3, 4, 5 and 6 numbers from the size of the sample space, to find the size of the event in question.)

Solution to Activity 19

(a) This is a first-order recurrence system, with parameters $a = 1$, $r = 2$ and $d = 1$.

(b) This is a first-order recurrence system, with parameters $a = 1$, $r = -1$ and $d = -1$.

(c) This is a first-order recurrence system, with parameters $a = 2$, $r = 1$ and $d = -1.5$. Since $r = 1$, the sequence specified is an arithmetic sequence.

(d) This is not a first-order recurrence system; that is, it is not a linear first-order constant-coefficient recurrence system. This is because the recurrence system is not linear, due to the presence of the squared term.

Solution to Activity 20

(a) Since $r = 2$, a closed form is

$$x_n = C \times 2^{n-1} + D$$

for some C, D that we need to work out. Now $x_1 = 3$ and $x_2 = 5$, so we have

$$3 = C + D,$$

$$5 = 2C + D.$$

Subtracting the first equation from the second gives $C = 2$. Then substituting in the first equation gives $D = 3 - 2 = 1$.

Therefore a closed form for the sequence is

$$x_n = 2 \times 2^{n-1} + 1$$
$$= 2^n + 1 \quad (n = 1, 2, 3, \ldots).$$

The fourth term is

$$x_4 = 2^4 + 1 = 17,$$

as expected, and the 10th term is

$$x_{10} = 2^{10} + 1 = 1025.$$

(b) Since $r = -\frac{1}{3}$, a closed form is

$$y_n = C \times (-\tfrac{1}{3})^{n-1} + D$$

for some C, D that we need to work out. Now $y_1 = 12$ and $y_2 = -3$, so we have

$$12 = C + D,$$
$$-3 = -\tfrac{1}{3}C + D.$$

Subtracting the second equation from the first gives $15 = \frac{4}{3}C$, that is, $C = \frac{45}{4}$. Then substituting in the first equation gives

$$D = 12 - \tfrac{45}{4} = \frac{48}{4} - \tfrac{45}{4} = \tfrac{3}{4}.$$

Therefore, a closed form for the sequence is

$$y_n = \tfrac{45}{4}(-\tfrac{1}{3})^{n-1} + \tfrac{3}{4} \quad (n = 1, 2, 3, \ldots).$$

The fourth term is

$$y_4 = \tfrac{45}{4}(-\tfrac{1}{3})^3 + \tfrac{3}{4} = \tfrac{1}{3},$$

as expected, and the 10th term is

$$y_{10} = \tfrac{45}{4}(-\tfrac{1}{3})^9 + \tfrac{3}{4} = 0.749 \text{ (to 3 d.p.)}.$$

(c) Since $r = -1$, a closed form is

$$z_n = C \times (-1)^{n-1} + D$$

for some C, D that we need to work out. Now $z_1 = 0$ and $z_2 = 2$, so we have

$$0 = C + D,$$
$$2 = -C + D.$$

Adding the two equations gives $2 = 2D$, or $D = 1$. Then substituting in the first equation gives $C = -1$. Therefore, a closed form for the sequence is

$$z_n = -(-1)^{n-1} + 1$$
$$= (-1)^n + 1 \quad (n = 1, 2, 3, \ldots).$$

The fourth term is

$$z_4 = (-1)^4 + 1 = 1 + 1 = 2,$$

as expected, and the 10th term is

$$z_{10} = (-1)^{10} + 1 = 1 + 1 = 2.$$

Solution to Activity 21

Since $r = 1.15$, a closed form is

$$P_n = C \times 1.15^{n-1} + D,$$

for some C, D that we need to work out. Now $P_1 = 6000$ and

$$P_2 = 1.15P_1 - 500 = 6400,$$

so we have

$$6000 = C + D,$$
$$6400 = 1.15C + D.$$

Subtracting the first equation from the second gives

$$400 = 0.15C, \qquad \text{or} \qquad C = \frac{400}{0.15} = \frac{8000}{3}.$$

Then substituting into the first equation gives

$$D = 6000 - \frac{8000}{3} = \frac{10\,000}{3}.$$

Therefore, a closed form for the sequence is

$$P_n = \tfrac{1}{3}\left(8000 \times 1.15^{n-1} + 10\,000\right) \quad (n = 1, 2, 3, \ldots).$$

The population size after 10 years (with $n = 11$) is given by

$$P_{11} = \tfrac{1}{3}\left(8000 \times 1.15^{10} + 10\,000\right)$$
$$= 14\,121.4873 = 14\,120 \text{ (to the nearest 10)}.$$

Hence the size of the deer population is estimated to be 14 120 after 10 years.

Solution to Activity 22

(a) We have $a = 100\,000$, $p = 0.05$ and $T = 20$. The annual repayment required is therefore

$$R = \frac{Lp(1+p)^T}{(1+p)^T - 1}$$
$$= \frac{100\,000 \times 0.05 \times 1.05^{20}}{1.05^{20} - 1}$$
$$= 8024.258\,719\ldots$$
$$= 8024.26 \text{ (to 2 d.p.)}.$$

Hence the annual repayment amount required is £8024.26, as stated in Subsection 3.1.

(b) If the borrower pays £8024.26 each year for 20 years, then the total amount paid is

$$20 \times £8024.26 = £160\,485.20.$$

Subtracting the amount of £100 000 originally borrowed (and eventually paid back in full), the total amount of interest paid by the borrower is £60 485.20.

Solution to Activity 23

The $n = 3$ case can be done in seven moves, as shown below.

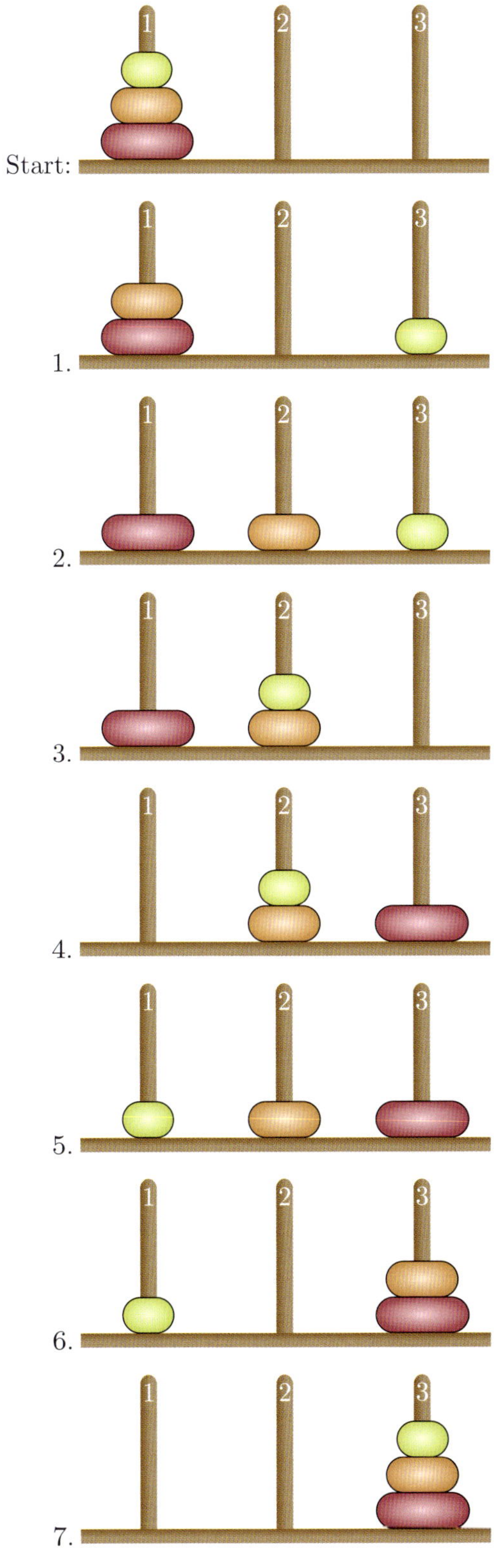

Solution to Activity 24

The first two terms of the sequence are $h_1 = 1$ and $h_2 = 3$. By the formula in the box on page 50, a closed form for the recurrence sequence is

$$h_n = C \times 2^{n-1} + D,$$

where C and D are constants that we need to find.

Substituting $h_1 = 1$ and $n = 1$, we obtain

$$1 = C + D,$$

while substituting $h_2 = 3$ and $n = 2$ gives

$$3 = 2C + D.$$

Subtracting the first of these simultaneous equations from the second gives

$$2 = C.$$

Substituting this value for C back into the first equation then gives

$$1 = 2 + D$$

so that

$$D = -1.$$

Hence a closed form for the sequence is

$$h_n = 2 \times 2^{n-1} - 1 \quad (n = 1, 2, 3, \dots),$$

and this can be simplified to

$$h_n = 2^n - 1 \quad (n = 1, 2, 3, \dots),$$

which is what was conjectured on page 58.

Solution to Activity 25

(a) Placing three circles in the plane divides it into 8 regions, as shown below. Thus $c_3 = 8$.

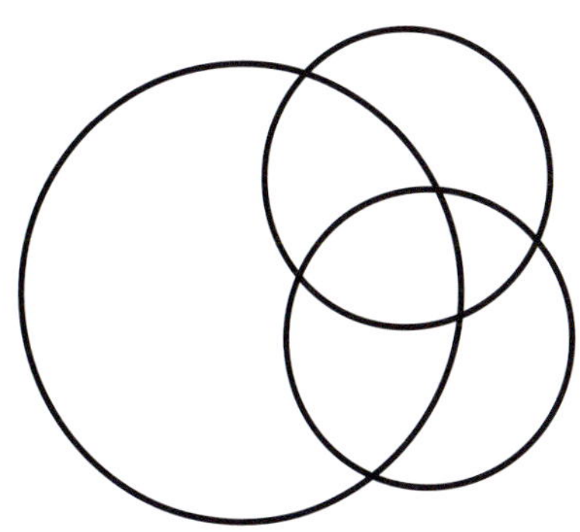

Since $c_1 = 2$, $c_2 = 4$ and $c_3 = 8$, a reasonable conjecture at this stage might be that $c_n = 2^n$.

(b) The picture below shows four circles drawn according to the conditions of the question. Counting the regions in the picture shows that $c_4 = 14$.

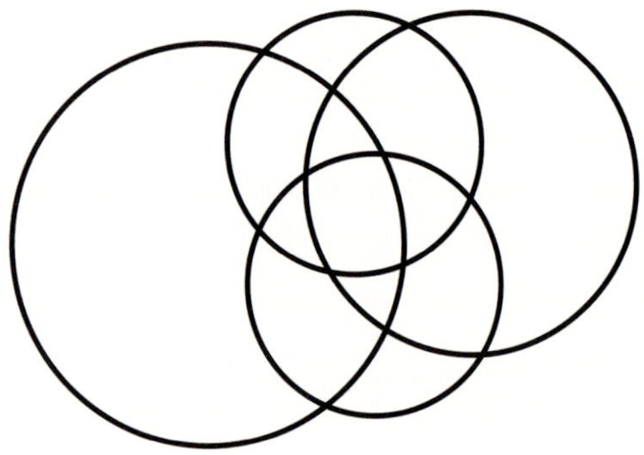

Thus the conjecture $c_n = 2^n$ is false when $n = 4$.

(c) Start with a plane with $n - 1$ circles placed on it, so that each pair of circles intersect in two places, but no three intersect at a point. Consider the effect of adding an nth circle to the plane, in such a way that it intersects each of the first $n - 1$ circles in two places, but does not pass through any of the existing intersection points. Since all of the intersection points with the new circle are distinct, there are $2(n - 1)$ such intersections.

Between each pair of consecutive intersection points on the new circle there is an arc of the circle. The case $n = 5$ is illustrated below, with the arcs numbered from 1 to 8.

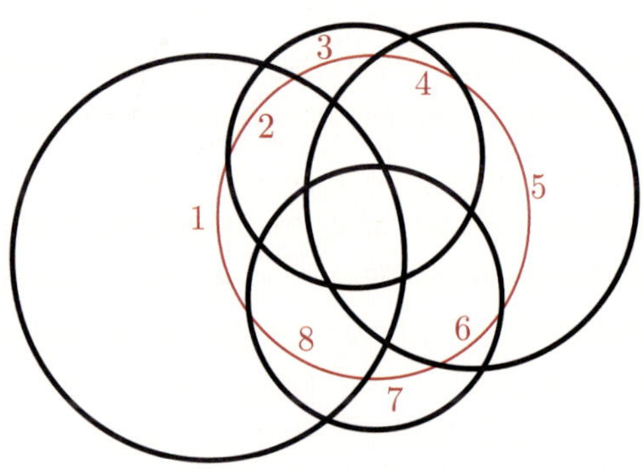

Since there are $2(n - 1)$ intersections, there are also $2(n - 1)$ arcs. Each arc divides one old region into two new ones, so there are $2(n - 1)$ old regions that are divided into two.

Therefore, adding the nth circle increases the number of regions by $2(n - 1)$, and so

$$c_n = c_{n-1} + 2(n - 1).$$

Note that $c_0 = 1$ and $c_1 = 2$, so this recurrence relation is not true for $n = 1$. Therefore, the recurrence system is

$$c_1 = 2, \quad c_n = c_{n-1} + 2(n - 1) \quad (n = 2, 3, 4, \dots).$$

(d) Starting from the initial condition $c_1 = 2$, we obtain:

$$c_2 = 2 + 2 = 4$$
$$c_3 = 4 + 4 = 8$$
$$c_4 = 8 + 6 = 14$$
$$c_5 = 14 + 8 = 22$$
$$c_6 = 22 + 10 = 32.$$

So 6 circles divide the plane into 32 regions.

Solution to Activity 26

(a) Clearly $x_1 = 1$, because the only one-letter sequence with an odd number of As is the sequence

A.

We can also list the 2-letter sequences containing an odd number of As, as follows:

$AB \quad AC \quad AD$

$BA \quad CA \quad DA.$

Hence $x_2 = 6$.

Similarly, $y_1 = 3$, since the one-letter sequences

$B \quad C \quad D$

all contain no As at all.

For y_2, we need to count the sequences that either contain two As (there is clearly only one of these) or no As at all (there are nine of these):

AA

$BB \quad CB \quad DB$

$BC \quad CC \quad DC$

$BD \quad CD \quad DD.$

Thus $y_2 = 10$.

(b) By the multiplication principle, there are a total of 4^n sequences of length n taken from the letters A, B, C, D, for $n \geq 1$.

Every sequence of length n that does not contain an odd number of As must either contain an even number of As, or no As. Hence by the subtraction principle we have

$$y_n = 4^n - x_n,$$

for $n \geq 1$.

(c) We want to count x_n, the number of sequences of n letters that contain an odd number of As. Consider the last letter of any such sequence. This must be one of A, B, C or D, so we can count x_n by separately counting four cases depending on the last letter, and then recombine the cases using the addition principle.

If the last letter is A, then the sequence of $n-1$ letters before this must contain either an even number of As or no As.

$$\underbrace{BDACAAB\cdots A}_{\substack{\text{sequence of length } n-1,\\ \text{even number of } As \text{ or no } As}} \quad A$$

Now there are y_{n-1} sequences of $n-1$ letters that contain either an even number of As or no As. Therefore, there are y_{n-1} sequences of n letters containing an odd number of As, where the last letter is A.

If the last letter is B, then the sequence of $n-1$ letters before this must contain an *odd* number of As.

$$\underbrace{BDACADB\cdots A}_{\substack{\text{sequence of length } n-1,\\ \text{odd number of } As}} \; B$$

There are x_{n-1} sequences of $n-1$ letters containing an odd number of As. Therefore, there are x_{n-1} sequences of n letters containing an odd number of As, where the last letter is B.

If the last letter is C or D, a similar argument to the case where the last letter is B applies. In both cases, there are x_{n-1} sequences of n letters containing an odd number of As.

Therefore

$$\begin{aligned} x_n &= y_{n-1} + x_{n-1} + x_{n-1} + x_{n-1} \\ &= y_{n-1} + 3x_{n-1}, \end{aligned}$$

as required.

(d) From part (b), we know that

$$y_{n-1} = 4^{n-1} - x_{n-1}.$$

Substituting this into the equation from part (c) gives

$$x_n = \left(4^{n-1} - x_{n-1}\right) + 3x_{n-1} = 2x_{n-1} + 4^{n-1}.$$

Since $x_1 = 1$, the recurrence system is

$$x_1 = 1, \quad x_n = 2x_{n-1} + 4^{n-1} \quad (n = 2, 3, 4, \ldots).$$

(e) Using the recurrence system found in part (d), we find

$$\begin{aligned} x_1 &= 1 \\ x_2 &= 2 \times 1 + 4^1 = 6 \\ x_3 &= 2 \times 6 + 4^2 = 28 \\ x_4 &= 2 \times 28 + 4^3 = 120 \\ x_5 &= 2 \times 120 + 4^4 = 496 \\ x_6 &= 2 \times 496 + 4^5 = 2016. \end{aligned}$$

Thus $x_6 = 2016$.

Solution to Activity 27

$F_{15} = 377 + 233 = 610$ and $F_{16} = 610 + 377 = 987$.

Solution to Activity 28

(a)

	u_0	u_1	u_2	u_3	u_4
(i)	1	2	4	8	16
(ii)	1	10	100	1000	10 000
(iii)	2	12	104	1008	10 016
(iv)	3	22	204	2008	20 016

(b) In sequence (i), the terms are powers of 2, so $u_n = 2^n$ is an appropriate conjecture.

In sequence (ii), the terms are powers of 10, so $u_n = 10^n$ is an appropriate conjecture.

(c) The terms of sequence (iii) are equal to the sum of the corresponding terms in sequences (i) and (ii). So, a conjecture for the nth term is $u_n = 2^n + 10^n$.

(d) The terms of sequence (iv) are equal to the sum of the corresponding terms in sequence (ii) and sequence (iii). Thus a conjecture for the nth term is $u_n = 2^n + 2 \times 10^n$.

(Alternatively, you could note that the terms in sequence (iv) are equal to the corresponding term in sequence (i), plus twice the corresponding term in sequence (ii), which leads to the same conjecture, $u_n = 2^n + 2 \times 10^n$.)

Solution to Activity 29

(a) The auxiliary equation is

$$r^2 - 4r + 4 = 0.$$

Since

$$r^2 - 4r + 4 = (r-2)(r-2) = (r-2)^2,$$

the solution to $r^2 - 4r + 4 = 0$ is $r = 2$.

This auxiliary equation has only one solution.

(The method used previously to find the general solution of a recurrence relation needed two solutions.)

(b)

	u_0	u_1	u_2	u_3	u_4
(i)	1	2	4	8	16
(ii)	0	2	8	24	64
(iii)	3	8	20	48	112

(c) For $n = 0, 1, 2, 3, 4$, the values of 2^n are $1, 2, 4, 8, 16$, which match the terms $u_0, u_1, \dots, u_4$ for sequence (i) in the table above.

Similarly, for $n = 0, 1, 2, 3, 4$, the values of $n \times 2^n$ are $0, 2, 8, 24, 64$, which match the terms u_0, u_1, u_2, u_3, u_4 for sequence (ii) in the table above.

(d) If $u_n = 2^n$, then $u_{n-1} = 2^{n-1}$ and $u_{n-2} = 2^{n-2}$, so

$$\begin{aligned} 4u_{n-1} - 4u_{n-2} &= 4 \times 2^{n-1} - 4 \times 2^{n-2} \\ &= 2 \times 2^n - 1 \times 2^n \\ &= 2^n \\ &= u_n, \end{aligned}$$

which shows that the sequence given by $u_n = 2^n$ satisfies the recurrence relation.

Similarly, if $u_n = n \times 2^n$, then

$$u_{n-1} = (n-1) \times 2^{n-1}$$

and

$$u_{n-2} = (n-2) \times 2^{n-2},$$

so

$$\begin{aligned} &4u_{n-1} - 4u_{n-2} \\ &= 4 \times (n-1) \times 2^{n-1} - 4 \times (n-2) \times 2^{n-2} \\ &= 2 \times (n-1) \times 2^n - (n-2) \times 2^n \\ &= (2n - 2 - n + 2) \times 2^n \\ &= n \times 2^n \\ &= u_n, \end{aligned}$$

which shows that the sequence given by $u_n = n \times 2^n$ satisfies the recurrence relation.

Now suppose that

$$u_n = A \times 2^n + B \times n \times 2^n,$$

where A and B are constants. Then

$$u_{n-1} = A \times 2^{n-1} + B \times (n-1) \times 2^{n-1},$$

and

$$u_{n-2} = A \times 2^{n-2} + B \times (n-2) \times 2^{n-2}.$$

It follows that

$$\begin{aligned} &4u_{n-1} - 4u_{n-2} \\ &= 4 \times A \times 2^{n-1} + 4 \times B \times (n-1) \times 2^{n-1} \\ &\qquad - 4 \times A \times 2^{n-2} - 4 \times B \times (n-2) \times 2^{n-2} \\ &= A(2 \times 2^n - 1 \times 2^n) \\ &\qquad + B(2 \times (n-1) \times 2^n - (n-2) \times 2^n) \\ &= A \times 2^n + B \times (2n - 2 - n + 2) \times 2^n \\ &= A \times 2^n + B \times n \times 2^n \\ &= u_n, \end{aligned}$$

which shows that the sequence given by $u_n = A \times 2^n + B \times n \times 2^n$ satisfies the recurrence relation, as required.

In sequence (iii), we have $u_0 = 3$ and $u_1 = 8$. Substituting $n = 0$ and $u_0 = 3$ into the equation for a closed form gives

$$3 = A \times 2^0 + B \times 0 \times 2^0,$$

so $A = 3$. Similarly, substituting $n = 1$ and $u_1 = 8$ gives

$$8 = A \times 2^1 + B \times 1 \times 2^1,$$

that is,

$$8 = 2A + 2B.$$

Since $A = 3$, this gives $B = 1$.

Solution to Activity 30

(a) The auxiliary equation is

$$r^2 - 7r + 12 = 0.$$

Factorising gives

$$(r-3)(r-4) = 0.$$

This has solutions $r = 3$ and $r = 4$.

Thus the general solution for the recurrence relation is

$$u_n = A \times 3^n + B \times 4^n,$$

where A and B are unknown constants.

To find A and B, we use the initial terms of the sequence, $u_0 = 2$ and $u_1 = 7$. Substituting $n = 0$ and $u_0 = 2$ into the general solution, we obtain

$$2 = A \times 3^0 + B \times 4^0,$$

so

$$A + B = 2.$$

Similarly, substituting $n = 1$ and $u_1 = 7$ gives

$$7 = A \times 3^1 + B \times 4^1,$$

that is

$$3A + 4B = 7.$$

Subtracting three times the first equation from the second gives $B = 1$. Then, substituting this value of B in the first equation gives $A = 1$. Thus a closed form for the given recurrence sequence is

$$u_n = 3^n + 4^n \quad (n = 0, 1, 2, \ldots).$$

(b) The auxiliary equation is

$$r^2 - 6r + 9 = 0.$$

Factorising gives

$$(r-3)^2 = 0.$$

This has the (repeated) solution $r = 3$.

Thus the general solution for the recurrence relation is

$$u_n = (A + Bn) \times 3^n,$$

where A and B are unknown constants.

To find A and B, we use the initial terms of the sequence, $u_0 = 2$ and $u_1 = 7$. Substituting $n = 0$ and $u_0 = 2$ into the general solution, we obtain

$$2 = (A + B \times 0) \times 3^0,$$

so $A = 2$.

Similarly, substituting $n = 1$ and $u_1 = 7$ gives

$$7 = (A + B \times 1) \times 3^1,$$

that is

$$3A + 3B = 7.$$

Substituting $A = 2$ into this equation then gives $B = \frac{1}{3}$. Thus a closed form for the given recurrence sequence is

$$u_n = (2 + \tfrac{1}{3}n) \times 3^n \quad (n = 0, 1, 2, \ldots).$$

(c) The auxiliary equation is

$$r^2 - 2r - 8 = 0.$$

Factorising gives

$$(r-4)(r+2) = 0.$$

This has solutions $r = 4$ and $r = -2$.

Thus the general solution of the recurrence relation is

$$x_n = A \times 4^n + B \times (-2)^n,$$

where A and B are unknown constants.

To find A and B, we use the initial terms of the sequence, $x_0 = 2$ and $x_1 = 7$. Substituting $n = 0$ and $x_0 = 2$ into the general solution, we obtain

$$2 = A \times 4^0 + B \times (-2)^0,$$

so

$$A + B = 2.$$

Similarly, substituting $n = 1$ and $x_1 = 7$ gives

$$7 = A \times 4^1 + B \times (-2)^1,$$

that is

$$4A - 2B = 7.$$

Adding twice the first equation to the second equation gives $6A = 11$, so $A = \frac{11}{6}$. Substituting this value of A in the first equation then gives $B = \frac{1}{6}$. Thus a closed form for the given recurrence sequence is

$$x_n = \tfrac{11}{6} \times 4^n + \tfrac{1}{6} \times (-2)^n \quad (n = 0, 1, 2, \ldots).$$

(d) The auxiliary equation is

$$r^2 + \tfrac{5}{2}r - \tfrac{3}{2} = 0;$$

that is,

$$2r^2 + 5r - 3 = 0.$$

Factorising gives

$$(2r-1)(r+3) = 0,$$

so the solutions are $r = \frac{1}{2}$ and $r = -3$.

Thus the general solution of the recurrence relation is

$$a_n = A \times \left(\tfrac{1}{2}\right)^n + B \times (-3)^n,$$

where A and B are unknown constants.

To find A and B, we use the initial terms of the sequence, $a_0 = 1$ and $a_1 = 3$. Substituting $n = 0$ and $a_0 = 1$ into the general solution, we obtain

$$1 = A \times \left(\tfrac{1}{2}\right)^0 + B \times (-3)^0,$$

so

$$A + B = 1.$$

Similarly, substituting $n = 1$ and $a_1 = 3$ gives

$$3 = A \times \left(\tfrac{1}{2}\right)^1 + B \times (-3)^1,$$

that is

$$\tfrac{1}{2}A - 3B = 3.$$

Adding three times the first equation to the second equation gives

$$\tfrac{7}{2}A = 6,$$

so $A = \frac{12}{7}$. Substituting this value of A into the first equation then gives

$$B = 1 - \tfrac{12}{7} = -\tfrac{5}{7}.$$

Thus a closed form for the given recurrence sequence is

$$a_n = \tfrac{12}{7} \times \left(\tfrac{1}{2}\right)^n - \tfrac{5}{7} \times (-3)^n \quad (n = 0, 1, 2, \ldots).$$

Solution to Activity 32

With $n = 20$, a calculator gives

$$\frac{\phi^{20}}{\sqrt{5}} = 6765.00003.$$

Thus, by Binet's approximation, $F_{20} = 6765$.

Solution to Activity 33

(a) Since the single-letter sequences A and B are the only ones possible, and neither contains consecutive occurrences of the letter A, we have $u_1 = 2$.

The sequences of length 2 that do not contain consecutive As are

$$AB \quad BA \quad BB.$$

Hence $u_2 = 3$.

(b) Take any valid sequence of n letters, and look at the nth letter in the sequence.

If this letter is B, then the first $n - 1$ letters of the sequence can be any sequence without consecutive As, and there are u_{n-1} of these:

$$\underbrace{BABBABA\cdots A}_{\substack{\text{Sequence of length } n-1,\\ \text{no consecutive } A\text{s}}}\ B$$

If the last letter is A, then the $(n - 1)$th letter cannot be A, so it must be B. The first $n - 2$ letters of the sequence can be any sequence without consecutive As, so there are u_{n-2} of these:

$$\underbrace{BABBAB\cdots A}_{\substack{\text{Sequence of length } n-2,\\ \text{no consecutive } A\text{s}}}\ BA$$

Thus, by the addition principle, the sequence satisfies the recurrence relation

$$u_n = u_{n-1} + u_{n-2},$$

which is the Fibonacci recurrence relation.

(c) The initial terms of the sequence (u_n) are $u_1 = 2$ and $u_2 = 3$, which are the third and fourth Fibonacci numbers F_3 and F_4. It follows that u_{10} is equal to F_{12}, which we can calculate using Binet's approximation with $n = 12$. A calculator gives

$$\frac{\phi^{12}}{\sqrt{5}} = 144.0014\ldots,$$

so $u_{10} = 144$.

Acknowledgements

Grateful acknowledgement is made to the following sources:

Figures 6 and 7: Adapted from:
http://www.texample.net/tikz/examples/towers-of-hanoi/

Page 5: www.CartoonStock.com

Page 56: www.CartoonStock.com

Page 60: Taken from: http://en.wikipedia.org/wiki/File:Elucas_1.png.
This file is licensed under the Creative Commons Attribution-Share Alike Licence http://creativecommons.org/licenses/by-sa/3.0/

Page 72: www.CartoonStock.com

Page 101: Adapted from:
http://www.texample.net/tikz/examples/towers-of-hanoi/

Every effort has been made to contact copyright holders. If any have been inadvertently overlooked the publishers will be pleased to make the necessary arrangements at the first opportunity.

Index